Harvard Semitic Monographs

Volume 4

THE COSMIC MOUNTAIN IN CANAAN AND THE OLD TESTAMENT

Richard J. Clifford

Harvard University Press

Cambridge, Massachusetts

1972

Library of Congress Catalog Card Number 71-188968

SBN 674-17425-9

Printed in the United States of America

For my parents

PREFACE

The present book is a total revision and expansion of a doctoral dissertation presented to Harvard University in 1970. The dissertation was directed by Professor Frank Moore Cross, Jr., to whom I am indebted for kind support and many helpful suggestions. Professors Thorkild Jacobsen and William L. Moran provided much assistance in Chapter I.

The Ugaritic texts are cited according to A. Herdner, *Corpus des tablettes en cunéiformes alphabétiques*, Paris, 1963, following the international convention requested by Professor D. O. Edzard. A synoptic table of the various systems of designating the texts is included at the end of the text. Texts not in the *Corpus* are designated by the volume of original publication, for example, *PRU*, II, *Ugaritica*, V.

I have departed from custom by attempting an approximate vocalization of the texts on the basis of transcriptions and comparative semitics. There are few certainties in the vocalization of Ugaritic, yet for the clearer picture it affords of the metrics and of the translator's understanding, I feel the attempt is worth making. Unless otherwise noted, all translations are my own.

R. J. Clifford, S.J.

Weston College School of Theology
Cambridge, Massachusetts
Autumn 1971

CONTENTS

THE COSMIC MOUNTAIN

IN CANAAN AND

THE OLD TESTAMENT

ABBREVIATIONS

Anal. Bibl.	Analecta Biblica
ANEP	*The Ancient Near East in Pictures*, 2nd ed.
ANET	*Ancient Near Eastern Texts*, 3rd ed.
BA	*The Biblical Archaeologist*
BAR	*The Biblical Archaeologist Reader*, 3 vols.
BASOR	*Bulletin of the American Schools of Oriental Research*
BK	Biblischer Kommentar
BZAW	Beihefte zur Zeitschrift für die Alttestamentliche Wissenschaft
CBQ	*The Catholic Biblical Quarterly*
CML	G. R. Driver, *Canaanite Myths and Legends*
CTA	*Corpus des tablettes en cunéiformes alphabétiques*, ed. A. Herdner
EA	J. A. Knudtzon, *Die El-Amarna Tafeln*
EUT	Marvin Pope, *El in the Ugaritic Texts*
FF	*Forschungen und Fortschritte*
HTR	*Harvard Theological Review*
HUCA	*Hebrew Union College Annual*
IDB	*The Interpreter's Dictionary of the Bible*
JAOS	*Journal of the American Oriental Society*
JBL	*Journal of Biblical Literature*
JCS	*Journal of Cuneiform Studies*
JNES	*Journal of Near Eastern Studies*

ABBREVIATIONS

JSS	*Journal of Semitic Studies*
KAI	H. Donner and W. Röllig, *Kanaanäische und Aramäische Inschriften*
KS	Otto Eissfeldt, *Kleine Schriften*
MIO	*Mitteilungen des Instituts für Orientforschung*
PRU	*Le Palais royal d'Ugarit*, 5 vols.
RB	*Revue Biblique*
RGG	*Die Religion in Geschichte und Gegenwart*, 3rd ed.
RHR	*Revue de l'Histoire des Religions*
RHPR	*Revue d'Histoire et de Philosophie Religieuses*
RS	*Ras Shamra*
TIT	Thorkild Jacobsen, *Toward the Image of Tammuz and Other Essays on Mesopotamian History and Culture*
UT	Cyrus Gordon, *Ugaritic Textbook*
VT	*Vetus Testamentum*
WM	*Wörterbuch der Mythologie*, ed. H. W. Haussig, vol. I
WUS	J. Aistleitner, *Wörterbuch der Ugaritischen Sprache*, 3rd ed.
ZA	*Zeitschrift für Assyriologie*
ZAW	*Zeitschrift für die alttestamentliche Wissenschaft*
ZDMG	*Zeitschrift der Deutschen Morgenländischen Gesellschaft*
ZDPV	*Zeitschrift des deutschen Palästina-Vereins*

INTRODUCTION

Myth in the Hebrew Bible has always been a topic of popular and scholarly interest. The rediscovery of the Ancient Near East on a scientific basis beginning in the nineteenth century revealed the myths of the cultures prior to and contemporary with the Bible. Numerous parallels to biblical lore were discovered in these newly understood literatures.[1] The presence of pagan myths or mythic motifs in the Bible gave rise to heated debate and also to mature reflection on the nature of myth and biblical reality.[2]

---

1. A useful summary in English of the *Religionsgeschichtlich* school that resulted from these discoveries is Herbert F. Hahn, *The Old Testament and Modern Research*, rev. ed. by Horace D. Hummel (Philadelphia: Fortress, 1966), pp. 83-118, 277-280. Also H. J. Kraus, *Geschichte der historisch-kritischen Erforschung des Alten Testament*, 2nd ed. (Neukirchen: Neukirchener Verlag, 1969), pp. 295-340.

2. The literature is enormous. A clear presentation of many of the modern problems of myth, with a bibliographical guide, is Avery Dulles, "Symbol, Myth, and the Biblical Revelation," *Theological Studies*, 27 (1966), 1-26. Important today is Claude Lévi-Strauss, in his

The present work takes one element in Ancient Near East religion--the cosmic mountain--and explores its meaning and function in Canaan and the Old Testament. The mountain in the other great civilizations will be presented insofar as they illuminate the same subject in Canaan and the Old Testament.[3]

Unfortunately, the term "cosmic mountain," as it has been used in the study of Ancient Near East religion, has been based in large measure on an assumed Mesopotamian *Weltberg*. The interpretation of Mesopotamian mythology, especially as it was worked out in the latter part of the nineteenth century in Germany, exerted considerable influence on the interpretation of the mythic fragments of the Bible and even of Ugaritic literature. The *Weltberg*, as it has been understood by an older generation of scholars, does not exist. Hence the term *Weltberg* or *Länderberg*,

---

Introduction to a Science of Mythology (New York: Harper, 1969). On Lévi-Strauss, see Edmund R. Leach, "Lévi-Strauss in the Garden of Eden: An Examination of Some Recent Developments in the Analysis of Myth," in *Transactions of the New York Academy of Sciences*, 23 (1961), 383-396. A later version of the same essay is "Genesis as Myth," in *Myth and Cosmos*, ed. John Middleton (Garden City, N.Y.: Doubleday, 1967), pp. 1-13.

3. There is need for systematic and detailed study of the cosmic mountain and center in the great Ancient Near East religions. For Egypt and Mesopotamia, there are only dated studies and scattered remarks in more recent works. For the Hittites and Hurrians, there is not, to my knowledge, any treatment at all.

which has come to be used of other ancient religions than Mesopotamian, must be used with extreme care.

I intend to clarify what is meant by cosmic mountain in Canaan and the Old Testament. In Canaan and in the Hebrew Bible, some mountains are given religious veneration. Certain texts and artistic works evidence the reason for the veneration paid to the mountains. These heights can be the meeting place of the gods, the source of water and fertility, the battleground of conflicting natural forces, the meeting place of heaven and earth, the place where effective decrees are issued. In these senses, the mountains are cosmic, that is, involved in the government and stability of the cosmos. The observations of phenomenology of religion on the cosmic mountain must constantly be specified and sharpened by analysis of the monuments of a particular culture.

In the Hebrew Bible, the cosmic mountain presents itself most dramatically in the beliefs surrounding Mount Zion. A hill between the Tyropoeon and Kidron valleys in Jerusalem, it is overshadowed in the east by the Mount of Olives and in the west by another mountain (today inaccurately called Mount Zion). This low and undistinguished mound is nonetheless called in the Bible the tallest mountain in the world, the place which God has chosen for his dwelling place, the place protected in a special way from enemies who can only stand at its base and rage, the place of battle where God's enemies will be defeated, the place where God dwells, where fertilizing streams come forth. Many years ago, it was recognized that mythic language was being employed in these descriptions of Mount Zion, though the mythic background was generally derived from Mesopotamia.[4] The Ugaritic tablets found at Ras Shamra since 1929 have enabled us to see more clearly the religious beliefs of the people of Syria-Palestine regarding the mountain. In contact with these people, Israel lived out her faith. The Canaanite storm-god, Baal-Hadad, lives on Mount Zaphon. Much of the lore concerning Ugaritic Zaphon is found to apply to Mount Zion as well. Zaphon, like Zion, is the scene of battle, is ultimately impregnable, is the place where the deity has his temple/palace and exercises kingship, and so on. Elements of Baal's mountain Zaphon in the Ugaritic myths have clearly attached themselves to Mount Zion in the Old Testament. Even Mount Sinai, the mountain of law-giving, stands in the Canaanite tradition of the cosmic mountain. Mutual light is cast on Canaanite and Israelite religions by comparing their traditions concerning sacred mountains.[5]

---

4. E.g., Hugo Gressmann in the second edition of *Die Religion in Geschichte und Gegenwart* (hereafter abbreviated as *RGG*), Tubingen: J. C. B. Mohr, 1929, I, 905, and Bernard Alfrink, "Der Versammlungsberg im äussersten Norden (Isa. 14)," *Biblica*, 14 (1933), 41-67, both writing before the full employment of Ugaritic material for comparison, seek parallels in the Mesopotamian world.

5. The Ugaritic material on the sacred mountain has begun to be exploited by Biblical scholars: H. Schmid, "Jahwe und die Kulttraditionen von Jerusalem," ZAW, NS, 26 (1955), 181; H. J. Kraus, *Psalmen*, BK XIII (Neukirchen: Neukirchener Verlag, 1966), esp. pp. 342-345; W. H. Schmidt, *Königtum Gottes in Ugarit und Israel*, 2nd ed., Beihefte zur Zeitschrift für die Alttestamentliche

Since the inspiration of the present investigation comes from observations of the school of phenomenology of religion, what that school or approach means by cosmic or sacred mountain must be examined. The holy mountain or cosmic mountain is usually studied under the larger heading of sacred space. Some mountains named in mythic and religious texts signify more than a mere geographical elevation. In the ancient civilizations from Egypt to India and beyond, the mountain can be a center of fertility, the primeval hillock of creation, the meeting place of the gods, the dwelling place of the high god, the meeting place of heaven and earth, the monument effectively upholding the order of creation, the place where god meets man, a place of theophany. The world view underlying such beliefs is variously explained by individual phenomenologists of religion. W. Brede Kristensen regards the mountain as the place where the life of the earth becomes most intense and tangible.[6] G. van der Leeuw sees the cosmic mountain as a "primal and permanent element of the world: out of the waters of chaos rose the

---

Wissenschaft (hereafter abbreviated as BZAW), 80 (Berlin: Alfred Töpelmann, 1966); Annemarie Ohler, *Mythologische Elemente im Alten Testament* (Dusseldorf: Patmos, 1969), pp. 154-173. None of these authors, however, has sufficiently recognized the different types of description of holy mountains within Ugaritic literature. I have attempted to do this in Chap. II.

6. *The Meaning of Religion*, trans. John B. Carman (The Hague: Martinus Nijhoff, 1960), pp. 106-109, 370-373.

primeval hill from which rose all life."[7] According to Mircea Eliade, the surrounding world was seen as a microcosm at the limits of which began the formless and chaotic. Every microcosm had a "center," a place sacred above all, where the sacred manifests itself in its totality. In cultures which have a heaven, earth, and hell, the mountain "center" is the axis along which these three cosmic areas are connected and where communion between them becomes possible.[8] The descriptions given are not necessarily mutually exclusive; they represent different emphases.

Basic to the interpretation of the cosmic mountain is an understanding of religious symbolism in the Ancient Near East. In the religions of the Ancient Near East, to characterize rather broadly, divine presence was sought not so much in a mystical inward searching of the soul but in symbolism where a relationship was established between the natural and supernatural worlds. By means of their form or shape, or some other indefinable quality, earthly objects symbolized or made present the gods or their abodes. The image "becomes" the reality. The

---

7. *Religion in Essence and Manifestation*, trans. J. E. Turner, with additions of 2nd German ed. (London: Allen & Unwin, 1938), pp. 55, 393-402.

8. *Images and Symbols*, trans. Philip Mairet (New York: Sheed & Ward, 1961), pp. 27-56; *Cosmos and History: The Myth of the Eternal Return*, trans. W. R. Trask (New York: Pantheon, 1959), pp. 1-48; *Patterns in Comparative Religion*, trans. Rosemary Sheed (New York: World, 1963), pp. 367-387; *RGG*, I, 1043.

cosmic mountain is an instance of this mode of thinking. The earthly mountain, even though it may be an insignificant hill, nonetheless because of its shape "is" the cosmic mountain.[9]

The rather massive assertions of the phenomenologists of religion about the elusive beliefs of ancient peoples are not of course susceptible to strict demonstration. Ancient myths and symbols are the products of long dead civilizations and are often preserved in languages that are only imperfectly understood. The phenomenologists grandly assume the psychic unity of mankind, an assumption which raises serious philosophical and psychological questions. Nonetheless, many of the assertions of the phenomenologists, such as the ones in the preceding two paragraphs, are verified in an examination of Ancient Near East religion.

This study, although employing, particularly as starting points, many of the insights of phenomenology of religion, will avoid the concepts "cosmic mountain" or "world-mountain" as defined by some phenomenologists of religion and scholars of the history of religions. The terms have become too vague and insufficiently based on textual analysis. The term "cosmic" and "cosmic mountain" and "cosmic center" will be used to designate more than a mere geographical location. It is a place set apart because of a divine presence or activity which relates to the world of man--ordering or stabilizing that world, acting upon it through natural forces, the point where

---

9. R. E. Clements, *God and Temple* (Oxford: Blackwell, 1965), pp. 1-17.

the earth touches the divine sphere. A more complete definition of "cosmic," however, must await the detailed examination of the evidence of the religions of the Ancient East, particularly of Canaan and Israel.

I. THE ANCIENT NEAR EASTERN BACKGROUND

The Cosmic Center in Mesopotamia

There exists no comprehensive modern study of the cosmic mountain or cosmic center in Mesopotamia. This chapter does not undertake a systematic study of the enormous and chronologically disparate mass of literary and artistic material from Mesopotamia. Rather, it only samples some instances of the cosmic center in Mesopotamian religious thought which may serve as illustration of the main subject: the cosmic mountain in Canaan and the Old Testament.

Sampling will be in two areas: (1) The cosmic center in cosmological speculation; and (2) the ideology of the ziqqurat.

It should be noted immediately that the concept of *Weltberg* or *Länderberg*, the world conceived as a huge mountain with heaven at the peak and the underworld at the base, once widely used by students of Mesopotamian thought,[1] is today seldom used. It is increasingly

---

1. E.g., by L. W. King, *Babylonian Religion and Mythology* (London, 1899), "Such a boat [used on the Tigris and Euphrates, no keel and circular] turned upside down would give a very accurate picture of the Babylonian

recognized that mountains simply were not central to the experience of the Mesopotamians. As was the case in Egypt, the mountain was at the border of the country, foreign, the source of enemy invasions. The European scholars who first undertook the difficult task of translating and interpreting Akkadian and Sumerian assumed the mountain in Mesopotamia was a place of grandeur and the scene of religious experience, as it was among the West Semites and other peoples. Peter Jensen, for example, in 1890, interpreted some uses of Sumerian *ḫursag* (= Akkadian *ḫuršānu*) as *Weltberg*.[2] Bruno Meissner in his detailed study of the beliefs of the Babylonians and Assyrians in 1925 assumed the existence of the *Weltberg* in describing the cosmology.[3] The concept began to lose favor, however. Edouard Dhorme in his *Les religions de Babylonie et d'Assyrie* in 1949 does not use the concept or

---

notion of the shape of earth, the base of which the sea encircled as a girdle encircles a man. To a dweller on the plains of Mesopotamia, the earth might well seem to be a mountain the centre of which was formed by the high mountain ranges of Kurdistan, while the Persian Gulf and the Indian Ocean which were on the Southeast of Babylonia, and the Red Sea and the Mediterranean lying to the Southwest and West respectively, doubtless led to the belief that the ocean surrounded the world" (pp. 29-30).

2. *Die Kosmologie der Babylonier* (Strasbourg, 1890), pp. 195-201.

3. *Babylonien und Assyrien* (Heidelberg: Carl Winter, 1925), pp. 107-111.

the term.[4] Dietz Otto Edzard in 1965, in dealing systematically with the mythology, is unwilling to commit himself on the cosmic mountain. He does admit that *duku*, Sumerian for "holy hill," is "a cosmic site," but does not explain further what this designation means.[5] Samuel Noah Kramer is one of the few modern scholars who uses the concept of the *Weltberg*, if not the name, in his study of Sumerian mythology. He writes, "It is not unreasonable to assume, therefore, that heaven and earth united were conceived as a mountain whose base was the bottom of the earth and whose peak was the top of the heaven."[6]

---

4. Paris: Presses Universitaires de France, 1949.

5. "Die Mythologie der Sumerer und Akkader," in *Götter und Mythen im Vorderen Orient, Wörterbuch der Mythologie*, ed. H. W. Haussig, vol. I (hereafter abbreviated as WM; Stuttgart: Ernst Klett, 1965), 17-140. Thorkild Jacobsen suggests that *duku* means "pure mound" and signifies basically a heap of grain, covered with mats and earth, a method of storage in use even today. Upon it, Enlil sits in the assembly in Nippur. (Private communication.)

6. *Sumerian Mythology*, rev. ed. (New York: Harper, 1961), p. 39. Kramer argues further in his book that Sumerian *kur*, "mountain," represents a cosmic concept. It is the "empty space between the earth's crust and the primeval sea," and is probably also the monster at the bottom of the "great below" (p. 76). Thorkild Jacobsen has argued convincingly against such a cosmic view of *kur* in his "Sumerian Mythology: A Review Article," *JNES*, 5

Most contemporary students, however, do not see the world as a mountain in explaining the Mesopotamian cosmology or, perhaps more accurately, do not bother to use the concept of *Weltberg*. Thorkild Jacobsen, for example, in discussing the same passage which drew forth Kramer's conclusions above, writes, "The Sumerian word *ḫursag* usually has reference to the range of mountains bordering the Mesopotamian plain on the east. As seen on the eastern horizon, its shining peaks towering from the earth up into heaven, the *ḫursag* appears indeed to belong equally to both of these cosmic entities, and the epithet here applied to it, 'of both heaven and earth,' is therefore as forceful as it is apt."[7] Jacobsen suggests that the one word *ḫursag* has a range of meanings. As the mountain range of Persia to the east, it is the area from which foreign invaders come. It is the land of the dead[8] and a place to be feared. The same word designates the rocky

---

(1946), 143-148, repr. in *Toward the Image of Tammuz and Other Essays on Mesopotamian History and Culture* (Cambridge, Mass.: Harvard, 1970), pp. 121-126 (hereafter abbreviated as *TIT*). J. van Dijk, *Sumerische Götterlieder*, Abhandlungen der Heidelberger Akademie der Wissenschaften, Phil.-Hist. Kl. 1960, 1 (Heidelberg: Carl Winter, 1960), II, 34, writes of "the holy hill upon the *Weltberg*, on which in primordial time the Anunna deities lived and on which agriculture, cattle-breeding, weaving, all that pertained to the civilization of Sumer, arose."

7. "Sumerian Mythology," p. 141; *TIT*, p. 118.

8. As in the idiom, *šadâ(šu) emēdu*, "to die," literally, "to push against one's mountain."

substratum of the topsoil in the north, a meaning to be discussed below in connection with *ḫuršānu* as ordeal. *Ḫursag* finally is the great stony desert to the west. The latter meaning is illustrated in a boundary list of Ur. The areas of *ŠID.TAB* and of Abiak, situated to the west of the Euphrates (although their exact location is not known), are bounded by *ḫur-sag-gá*. *Ḫursag* can scarcely be "mountain" in this text. It must be the stony desert to the west. This interpretation is strengthened by evidence that Ur in the time of Ibbi-Sin (ca. 1972-1947 B.C.) built a fort *bàd-igi-ḫur-sag*, "fortress facing the hursag," to keep out the Martus coming from the desert.[9] The basic meaning, then, of *ḫursag* seems to be the stony, rocky ground as it is found in the mountains of the east and as it comes out in the vast gravelly and stony desert to the west, contrasting so sharply with the alluvial soil of Sumer proper.[10]

---

9. The boundary list was published by F. R. Kraus, "Provinzen des neusumerisches Reiches von Ur," ZA, NS, 17 (1955), 45-75. The place name *igi-ḫur-sag-gá* was already known. In his article, "The Reign of Ibbi-Suen," JCS, 7 (1953), 41; TIT, p. 117, Jacobsen has offered the correction, *bàd-igi-ḫur-sag-gà*, "fortress facing the *ḫursag*." The interpretation of the boundary list is Jacobsen's. (Private communication.)

10. Jacobsen, "Babylonia and Assyria. V. Religion," *Encyclopaedia Britannica* (Chicago: Encyclopaedia Britannica, 1970), II, 975; *TIT*, p. 30. This understanding of *ḫursag* enables one to see how an older generation of scholars could see the world as a mountain. The *ḫursag*

The cosmic center plays a role in cosmological speculation. There is no myth in Sumerian which makes the creation of the world and of man its main theme. There are only hints in myths concerning other topics. In the poem called by Kramer, "The Creation of the Pickax," we have a valuable glimpse of a cosmology.[11]

> The lord did verily produce the normal order,
> The lord whose decisions cannot be altered,
> Enlil, did verily speed to remove Heaven from Earth,
> So that the seed (from which grew) the nation could
> sprout (up) from the field;
> Did verily speed to bring the Earth out from (under)
> Heaven (as a) separate (entity)
> (And) bound up for her (i.e. for Earth) the gash in
> the "bond of Heaven and Earth"
> So that the "flesh producer" could grow the vanguard
> (of mankind).

The "flesh producer" (*uzu-è*) is called in a variant the "(place where) flesh sprouted forth." The place referred to is the center of the temple of Inanna in Nippur. The reason for the sacred character of the place is that in primeval times the earth produced mankind there. Commemorated there was the wound and the severed bond, perhaps the navel string, caused by Enlil's separation of Heaven

---

is indeed the area on which the people of Mesopotamia lived, not as on a mountain but as on a rocky surface or subsurface.

11. S. N. Kramer translates in *Sumerian Mythology*, pp. 52-53. Jacobsen has made important corrections in "Sumerian Mythology," pp. 135-137; TIT, pp. 111-112.

and Earth. The name of the temple area was *Dur-an-ki*, "the bond of Heaven and Earth." In *Dur-an-ki*, after the wound had been closed, grew the first men like plants from the soil. It appears from the name given in the myth that the temple was a link between a heaven and an earth that had originally been one.[12] Nippur was a cosmic center, though not a mountain.

---

12. The names of other temples seem to confirm this. At Babylon was the temple *É-temenanki*, "The House, Foundation Platform of Heaven and Earth"; Assur, "House, the Mountain of the Universe"; Larsa, "House, Link of Heaven and Earth." However, one should not deduce too much from names alone. Many names appear to describe the impression of the beholder. "Link of Heaven and Earth" could mean simply that a lofty temple complex rising high into the heavens from a flat plain appeared to the beholder to be reaching to the heavens.

A serious problem is posed by some Sumerian temple hymns, excerpts from which are printed below. Is the language of these hymns mere description of the impression on the worshipper in the temple, or a description of the theology of the temple? "Eunir, which has grown high (uniting) heaven and earth, Foundation of heaven and earth, 'Holy of Holies,' Eridu, Abzu, shrine, erected for its prince." Eunir is a ziqqurat, TH no. 1, p. 17; "House, which extends over the midst of the sea, built on a holy place," TH no. 23, p. 33; "Your foundations (are like those of) the Abzu, fifty in number, 'seven' oceans (are within you)," TH no. 8, p. 23; "Uruku(g), shrine which causes the seed to come forth, belonging to the

A more complete cosmogony is preserved in the Akkadian epic *Enūma eliš* which indicates that Babylon as well as Nippur was a cosmic center. Four passages are of interest because they illustrate a view of the dwelling of the god and the center.

Ea, the god of wisdom, binds and slays Apsu, the fresh waters. He then establishes his dwelling upon Apsu and names it "Apsu."

> Having thus upon Apsu established his dwelling (*šubatsu*),
> He laid hold on Mummu, holding him by the nose-rope.
> After Ea had vanquished and trodden down his foes,
> Had secured his triumph over his enemies,
> In his sacred chamber in profound peace had rested.
> He names it "Apsu," for shrines he assigned (it).

---

holy An, called by a god name, within you (is) the river of ordeal (*i*$_7$*-lú-ru-gú*)," TH no. 21, p. 31. Åke W. Sjöberg and E. Bergmann, *The Collection of Sumerian Temple Hymns* (Locust Valley, N.Y.: J. J. Augustin, 1969). In the Keš Temple Hymns, "Temple, whose platform is suspended from heaven's midst, Whose foundation fills the Abzu," p. 169; "Temple, at its top a mountain, at its bottom a spring," p. 170; "Temple, foundation of the country, fierce ox of Aratta, Keš temple, foundation of the country, fierce ox of Aratta, Growing up like a mountain, embracing the sky. Growing up like Ekur when it lifts its head in the land, springing up like the Abzu, making its mountain green," pp. 167-168, in Gene B. Gragg, *The Keš Temple Hymns* (Locust Valley, N.Y.: J. J. Augustin, 1969).

In that same place his cult hut he founded.[13]

Ea founds his house upon the vanquished body of water, Apsu. He gives his new dwelling the name "Apsu." The location of his house upon Apsu, and its name suggest its function in the cosmos. The dwelling of the victorious Ea commemorates the victory over Apsu and perhaps in so commemorating it keeps in check the sweet waters under the earth.[14]

It is now possible, thanks to new finds and the proper placement of tablets already known, to add considerably to the account of Marduk's creation in Tablet V of *Enūma eliš*.[15] In Tablet IV, Marduk creates an ordered cosmos of the carcass of Tiamat. He measures the heavens to equal Abzu. Then, he makes Esharra correspond, ll. 140-146. Tablet V continues Marduk's work of creation.

---

13. Tablet I, 71-77. Trans. E. A. Speiser in *Ancient Near Eastern Texts* (Princeton, N.J.: Princeton University, 1969), p. 61. Hereafter abbreviated as *ANET*.

14. There is a possible Old Testament parallel in Psalms 29:10, *Yhwh lammabbûl yāšab*, "Yahweh is enthroned on the Flood." A similar idea may be expressed in a new text from Ugarit, *baʿlu yāṯibu kī ṯibtu ǵūru/Haddu rā* [*iyu*] *kī m-d-b*, "Baal is enthroned, yea, (his) seat is the mountain,/Haddu shepherds, yea (his seat is) the ocean (?)." *Ugaritica*, V (Paris: Imprimerie Nationale, 1968), 3.1-2 (*RS* 24.245, p. 557).

15. B. Landsberger and J. V. Kinnier Wilson, "The Fifth Tablet of *Enūma eliš*," *JNES*, 20 (1961), 154-179.

> He laid down her [text: his] head, heaped a mountain
> upon it,
> Opened up such a spring that a torrent could be
> drawn off,
> Then released through her eyes the Euphrates and
> Tigris,
> Closed up her nostrils, reserved the water,
> He heaped up high mountains at her udder,
> Drilled fountains (through the deep) to carry off
> the fountainhead.[16]

One should note here the juxtaposition of source of water and mountain. One is reminded of the West Semitic description of the dwelling of El, on the mountain at the source of the two rivers.

Further on in the same tablet, Marduk, intent on winning the gods' goodwill and permanent kingship for himself, provides a station for the gods in Babylon. The gods were previously confined to the Abzu. Now, Babylon has become a stopping place halfway between heaven and the Abzu. Marduk addresses the Igigi and the Anunnaki:

> Above the Apsu, where you have (hitherto) been residing,

---

16. Ibid., p. 161. Thorkild Jacobsen has suggested that the parts of Tiamat's body correspond to geographical realities. The eyes are the source of the two rivers in Anatolia. The udders or dugs are the tributaries arising in the Persian mountains. Both eyes and dugs are sources of fluid in the body. (Private communication.)

A counterpart (*mi-iḫ-rit*) of Esharra, which I have built above you,
Down below, I have hardened the soil for a building plot,
I shall build a habitation--my (most) charming abode!
Therein will I found its holy district,
I will install sleeping quarters, will establish my kingship.
When from the Apsu you go up for the Assembly,
There will be your night's resting(-place) to receive all of you;
When from the heavens you come down from the Assembly,
There will be your night's resting(-place) to receive all of you.
I shall call its name Babylon, "the homes of the great gods";
I shall build it with the craftsmanship [of the mas]ters!"[17]

Here clearly the earthly abode is the counterpart (*meḫret*)[18] of the heavenly abode. The earthly copy, Babylon,

---

17. Landsberger and Wilson, "The Fifth Tablet," pp. 165-167, ll. 119-130, except that we follow Jacobsen's suggestion of "sleeping quarters" for *kummu* instead of Landsberger's and Wilson's "holy chambers." (Private communication.)

18. W. L. Moran, "A New Fragment of *DIN.TIR.KI* = *Bābilu* and *Enūma Eliš* vi 61-66," *Studia Biblica et Orientalia*. Analecta Biblica, 16 (Rome: Pontifical Biblical Institute, 1959), 262. Hereafter abbreviated Anal. Bibl.

is also the stopping place of the gods on their way to and from the cosmic regions of Apsu and the heavens. On the cosmic waters Apsu, Marduk raises the structure which is a cosmic center uniting the heavenly and the earthly. The house of Marduk as the union of the upper and the lower is an appropriate meeting place for the gods of the heavenly and the (under)earthly regions. The gods do not meet on a mountain, as is the case among the West Semites, but on level ground, in a corner of the courtyard.

In Tablet VI, Marduk has a temple built for him as a monument of his victory. He requests the Anunnaki to build it "like that of lofty (?) Babylon, whose building you have requested, let its brickwork be fashioned," that is, there is to be a correspondence between the heavenly temple of Marduk and the earthly temple area (Esangil) in Babylon.

> When the second year arrived,
> Of Esangil, the counterpart (*meḫret*) of Apsu, they raised high the top;
> They built the lofty ziqqurat of the Apsu (Esangil),
> For Marduk, Enlil, and Ea, they established his temple (*bītašu*) as a dwelling (*šubta*).
> Majestically in their presence did he take their seat,
> And its "horns" were gazing at the foundations of Esharra.[19]

---

19. Landsberger and Wilson, "The Fifth Tablet," p. 177. On the problem of this passage, consult W. L. Moran, "A New Fragment," pp. 257-265.

The temple raised to the victorious Marduk seems to unite Apsu and the heavenly sphere.

The temple appears therefore to be part of the structure of the universe. Its base reaches into the underworld and its top to the heavens. It is a cosmic center. The well-known ancient map of the world on a clay tablet reflects the same view, that Babylon is the center of the world. In the map, Babylon is at the center of a world conceived as a disk.[20]

Caution is necessary in seeing cosmic significance in everything that has roots in the underworld and its top in the heavens. In some texts, these "cosmic" characteristics are applied to gods, temple, a god's net, a mythical tree, a mountain. The idea of greatness is simply expressed in terms of filling the whole universe.[21]

André Parrot in *Ziqqurats et Tour de Babel* has sketched the history of modern interpretation of the ziqqurat, the temple tower of Mesopotamia. Of modern theories, he lists four: that the ziqqurat is a tomb of the gods or kings; that it has a cosmological and symbolical significance; that it is a throne of the god and a true altar; that it is a gigantic base for the support of a sanctuary which is the habitation of a god and the place

---

20. As pictured, e.g., in Jean-Claude Margueron, *Mesopotamia*, trans. H. S. B. Harrison, *Archeologia Mundi* (New York: World, 1965), facing p. 93.

21. W. G. Lambert, *Babylonian Wisdom Literature* (Oxford: Clarendon, 1960), p. 327, with texts. For the mountain text, Gilgamesh Epic, Tablet IX, ii, 4-5, *ANET*, p. 88.

from which the god could descend to the temple at the base of the tower.[22]

It is characteristic of a religious symbol, especially one so imperfectly known as the ziqqurat, that more than one interpretation could be valid. We can exclude at once the view that it was a king's tomb as relying on a false analogy with the Egyptian pyramid. The fact that it was not a god's tomb will appear below. The other views find some support in the texts and architecture.

As H. W. F. Saggs has pointed out, the most common view until recently has been that of W. Andrae. He assumed that there were always two temples closely associated with a ziqqurat, one on the top and the other at the base. The "high temple" (*Hochtempel*) was the residence proper of the deity who at appropriate times came down to the low temple (*Tieftempel*). The absence of the lower temple in some ziqqurats shows that the ziqqurat was more than a mere passageway from higher to lower temple. Rather, the ziqqurat itself was a dwelling. The god lived there as can be seen from the fact that he had his bedroom there which was kept dark so that he could sleep. An actual cult was carried on in the temple on the top. The god left this higher temple to hold court in his "working quarters" on the ground below.[23]

---

22. Paris: Michel, 1949, pp. 202-217. An English abridgement is contained in the same author's *The Tower of Babel*, trans. E. Hudson (New York: Philosophical Library, 1955), pp. 57-64.

23. Summary in H. W. F. Saggs, *The Greatness That*

The ziqqurat has sometimes been interpreted as the mountain in which Marduk was imprisoned during the New Year Festival at Babylon. Heinrich Zimmern in 1918 interpreted KAR 143 as a *Kultkommentar* and a witness to the disappearance of Marduk into the *ḫuršānu*, which he translated as "mountain." The *ḫuršānu* was seen by him as *die unterirdische Gerichtstätte* and the *Totenreiche*.[24] Henri Frankfort in his well-known *Kingship and the Gods* in 1948 followed Zimmern's interpretation and stressed that the ziqqurat was the mountain, the realm of death where Marduk was confined until his liberation.[25] Wolfram von Soden in 1955 showed that *ḫuršān* does not mean "Weltberg, worin die Unterwelt sich befindet," as Zimmern and others had believed, but *Ordalstätte*.[26] So Marduk in this ritual is not imprisoned in a mountain (the ziqqurat) but rather undergoes some kind of ordeal.

We must look more closely at *ḫuršānu*. The two major modern Akkadian dictionaries both treat *ḫuršānu* as two words, "mountain (area)," and "the place of the river

---

Was Babylon (London: Sidgewick & Jackson, 1962), pp. 354-357, 523.

24. "Zum babylonischen Neujahrfest. Zweiter Beitrag." *Berichte...der Sächsischen Gesellschaft der Wissenschaften* 70, pt. 5 (1918), 3, n. 2., and *Das babylonische Neujahrfest*, Der Alte Orient 25, 3 (Leipzig: J. C. Hinrichs, 1926).

25. Chicago: Univ. of Chicago, 1948, pp. 321-325.

26. "Gibt es ein Zeugnis dafür, dass die Babylonier an die Wiederauferstehung Marduks geglaubt haben?" *ZA*, NS, 17 (1955), 140-141.

ordeal; the ordeal (itself)," and make no effort to show any relation between the two meanings.[27] Von Soden, it is true, elsewhere admits that *ḫuršānu* in its meaning of ordeal, place of ordeal linguistically cannot be separated from the Sumerian *ḫurš/sānu*, "mountain." His own suggestion that the river ordeal was called "mountain" euphemistically because those involved could only think with terror of the bottomless deep water, has little to commend it.[28]

A more convincing suggestion is that of Thorkild Jacobsen who joins the two meanings "river ordeal" and "rock substratum in the north." *Ḫuršānu* as "river ordeal" occurs only in Assyria, where the swift Tigris can be seen to increase in turbulence and speed by being forced through narrow rock channels (*ḫuršānu*). The river in the ordeal was divinized and made the judge. The god, River, was thought to be most forceful and discerning when the current was most powerful. The power was supplied by the rock channels. Hence the name *ḫuršānu* for both the river ordeal and the rocky channel which supplied the divine power to the river is most appropriate.[29]

---

27. *The Assyrian Dictionary* (Chicago: Univ. of Chicago, 1956) and W. von Soden, *Akkadisches Handwörterbuch* (Wiesbaden: Harrassowitz, 1965), *sub voce*.

28. Von Soden, "Gibt es ein Zeugnis?" p. 141.

29. Sumerian *i₇-lú-ru-gú*, lit. "river which flows against man," is the name for the river ordeal practiced at Uruk and Ur. It appears to be the functional equivalent of the northern *ḫuršānu*, "river ordeal." (Private communication of Thorkild Jacobsen.) References to texts

In summary, many modern scholars seem disinclined to use the concept of the *Weltberg* to describe Mesopotamian speculation about the cosmic center. Nonetheless, there is a cosmic center, where heaven and earth are united. The cosmic center appears in some texts to be commemorated by a shrine or temple. This can be verified for Nippur and Babylon. The ziqqurat is primarily the dwelling of the god. *Ḫuršān* describes the eastern mountains, the rock substratum in the north, as well as the stony western desert. As the rocky channel in which the Tigris River appears to become swift, the word appropriately designates the river ordeal as well as a mountain.

The Mountain in Egypt

Egypt, like Mesopotamia, was a flat land. The only mountains were off in the distance, at the horizon's edge. The Egyptian words for "mountain" and "highlands" signify what is desert and foreign. Nonetheless, in the view of a number of students of Egyptian religion, the mountain or hill, the *Urhügel* or primal hill, did figure in the beliefs of the Egyptians. Here creation took place.[30]

---

dealing with the *i₇-lú-ru-gú* can be found in Å. W. Sjöberg and E. Bergmann, *Sumerian Temple Hymns*, pp. 60-61.

30. John A. Wilson, "Egypt," in *Before Philosophy* (Hammondsworth: Penguin, 1949), pp. 59-61; Siegfried Morenz, *Ägyptische Religion* (Stuttgart: Kohlhammer, 1960), pp. 44-47; Hans Bonnet, "Urhügel," *Reallexikon der Ägyptischen Religionsgeschichte* (Berlin: De Gruyter, 1952), pp. 847-848. These treatments owe much to A. de Buck,

The view that connects hillock with creation has been plausibly derived from the Egyptian experience of the sinking of the annual flood waters and the emergence of the first isolated peaks of mud, refreshed with new fertile silt and rich with new life. These are appropriate sites for the creator god. In the popular seventeenth chapter of the Book of the Dead, Atum says

> I am Atum when I was alone in Nun [the waters of chaos from which life arose]; I am Re in his (first) appearance, when he began to rule that which he had made. Who is he? This "Re, when he began to rule that which he had made" means that Re began to appear as a king, as one who was before the liftings of the Shu had taken place [before the air god had lifted heaven apart from earth], when he was on the hill which is in Hermopolis...[31]

Amun-Re began creation on the primeval hillock arising out of the waters of chaos, Nun. In this version, the hillock is located in the ancient cult center Hermopolis. This middle Egyptian city gained the reputation of being the *Urstätte* in Egypt and attracted all the cosmogonic myths, of the primal hill, of the island of fire, and of the god in the lotus blossom. Other cities

---

De egyptische voorstellingen betreffende den oerheuvel, published in 1922. Some scholars deny that little islands of mud would have suggested mountain or hill to the Egyptians, for whom mountains played so small a role.

31. John A. Wilson, *ANET*, pp. 3-4. The bracketed notes and interpretations are Wilson's.

found it to their advantage to claim that they were the primal hill, or, as the Egyptians expressed it, "the holy places of the first time."

The belief in Osiris seems to have contributed to the idea of the *Urhügel*. Ancient tradition places Osiris' grave on an island which is seen as a holy hill. Osiris not only is interred in the hill but, rising to life, he is enthroned upon it. The hill, at once grave and throne, is to be located at the temple of Seti I at Abydos.[32]

Whether temples in Egypt marked the site of creation and participated in the structure of the universe, as seems to have been the case in Mesopotamia, may be doubted. The simplicity of the early shrines argues against any elaborate mythical interpretation of their significance. It should be noted, though, that the temple of On was on an artificial hill which was called "high sand in On" and may have been an image of the primal hill.[33] The elaborate symbolism which in the course of time was applied to the temple seems to have been the result of a kind of scholastic speculation which had little to do with the temple's actual function in daily religion. The temple, in these speculations, becomes a microcosm of the universe. The roof is the roof of heaven and is painted blue with stars and gods in the form of birds. The floor comes to be the earth from which the marsh plants which decorate the base of the walls spring up.[34]

---

32. Bonnet, "Urhügel," p. 848.

33. Ibid., p. 847.

34. Harold H. Nelson, "The Egyptian Temple," *The*

Regarding the possible symbolic meaning of the pyramid, Egyptologists differ according to whether they stress the architectural development from the mastaba[35] or the symbolism or the pyramidal shape.[36] The British Egyptologist I. E. S. Edwards lays great stress on the symbolic when he writes: "It is not difficult to imagine that the mound, although purely practical in origin, was thought to resemble the hill which had emerged from the primeval waters when the earth came into being and thus represented existence. Death could be magically countered by the presence of this potent symbol."[37]

Egypt seems to have influenced Canaan in the area of mountain symbolism not at all. The Egyptian experience of the primal hill of creation was unique to herself--

---

Biblical Archaeologist Reader, 3 vols. (Garden City, N.Y.: Doubleday, 1961), I, 150-152 (hereafter abbreviated as *BAR*); Serge Sauneron, "Temples," in Georges Posener, *A Dictionary of Egyptian Civilization* (London: Methuen, 1962), p. 282; Hans Bonnet, "Tempel," *Reallexikon*, pp. 786-787; Henri Frankfort, *Ancient Egyptian Religion* (New York: Columbia Univ., 1948), pp. 153, 156.

35. L. Borchhardt, *Die Entstehung der Pyramide an der Baugeschichte der Pyramide bei Majdum nachgewiesen* (Berlin: Springer, 1928).

36. J. H. Breasted, *Development of Religion and Thought in Ancient Egypt* (New York: C. Scribner's Sons, 1912), p. 72. I. E. S. Edwards, *The Pyramids of Egypt* (Hammondsworth: Penguin, 1949), pp. 232-241, and also in *A Dictionary of Egyptian Civilization*, pp. 232-233.

37. *A Dictionary of Egyptian Civilization*, p. 233.

the result of her peculiar geography. Her temple and pyramid ideology appear to be proper to herself.

Egypt offers some evidence that the primal hill is the center of the cosmos, that life arises there and spreads outward. As such, it is akin to what phenomenology of religion calls a "cosmic center." It is not certain at all whether or in what manner temples, obelisks, and pyramids were related to the primal hill. There is no evidence of direct influence of the Egyptian conception upon the Canaanite cosmic mountain.

The Cosmic Mountain among the Hurrians and Hittites

In contrast to Mesopotamia and Egypt, mountains are a prominent feature of Anatolia and in some of the areas inhabited by the Hurrians. They played a significant role in the religious thought of the peoples of the area. Yet little scholarly attention has been directed toward the sacred mountain and its special place in Hittite and Hurrian religion.

One would expect mutual influence among the Canaanites, the Hittites, and the Hurrians. The Hittites, particularly during the time of the Empire, came into close contact with Syria. At Ugarit, official correspondence between that city and the Hittite court has been discovered. Hittite religion is strongly syncretistic and open to foreign influence, mixing Proto-Khattic, Hurrian, and Akkado-Sumerian gods and myths in a bewildering fashion.

In 1953, a Canaanite myth from Boghazköy, telling of intrigue between El-kunirsha, Ashertu, and the

Storm-god, was first published.[38] Another myth, published earlier, also is Canaanite in origin--that of Ishtar and Mount Pišaiša. The exact location of the mountain is unknown, but it is mentioned among the divinized mountains Lebanon and Hermon in treaties. In our fragment, the mountain sleeps with Ishtar, obviously against her will. Ishtar becomes angry and the mountain falls down before her to beg for mercy. In verse 17, there is reference to a victory of the Storm-god over Sea (*dAruna*).[39]

---

38. Heinrich Otten, "Ein kanaanäischer Mythus aus Boğasköy," *Mitteilungen des Instituts für Orientforschung*, 1 (1953), 125-150. English translation by Albrecht Goetze, *ANET*, p. 519. This fragment shows El-kunirsha living in his tent.

39. H. G. Güterbock, *Kumarbi* (New York: Europa-Verlag, 1946), p. 122, and Otten, "Ein kanaanäischer Mythus," 147-148. Emmanuel Laroche has published in transcription a critical edition of all the myths in Hittite (except the already critically edited Epic of Ullikummi). Among the myths of foreign origin, he lists the mythic fragments, "Purification (?) de Baal," "Baal exorcisé," "Kumarbi, Ea, et l'Ocean," and "Combats de Baal," *Revue Hittite et Asianique*, 23 (1965), 63-178, and 26 (1968), 121-204. A translation by Laroche is promised in the series *Littératures anciennes du Proche Orient*, Editions du Cerf, Paris. On the basis of his edition and forthcoming translation, we may expect increased attention paid to the relationship between Hittite and Canaanite myth.

The Hurrians, as well as the Hittites, exercised great influence in Syria-Palestine. Hurrian apparently became the principal spoken language in Tunip, Qatna, and Alalakh. The Egyptian designation of Palestine is Ḫuru. Uriah the "Hittite" and the Jebusites of Jerusalem were apparently Hurrian.[40] At Ugarit, many Hurrian documents have been found, including many of a religious nature. The Hurrians served as intermediaries between foreign religion and the Hittites. The way of borrowing went from Syria via Cilicia, where Hurrian scribal schools flourished, to the Hittite capital.[41] Apparently the Canaanite myths, mentioned above, went into Anatolia through the Hurrians. The complete loss of parallelism in the myth of El, Ashertu, and the Storm-god precludes direct borrowing, and the mention of the Mala River (= Euphrates) in Hurrian territory, indicates that the Hurrians were the mediators.

It is not easy to be definite regarding the mountain in Anatolian religion. Teshub was the chief figure in the Hurrian pantheon and the Storm-god, who was identified with Teshub, was also the leading deity among the

---

40. E. A. Speiser, "The Hurrian Participation in the Civilizations of Mesopotamia, Syria, and Palestine," *Journal of World History*, 1 (1953), 311-327, repr. in *Oriental and Biblical Studies*, ed. J. J. Finkelstein and Moshe Greenberg (Philadelphia: Univ. of Pennsylvania, 1967), pp. 244-269.

41. H. G. Güterbock, "Hittite Mythology," *Mythologies of the Ancient World*, ed. S. N. Kramer (Garden City, N.Y.: Doubleday, 1961), p. 143.

Hittites. Like Syrian Hadad, he was equipped as a warrior. In the late iconography, he came to assume some of the characteristics of Hadad. One of the most impressive pictures of the Storm-god is at the rock shrine of Yazilikaya where he stands on two divinized mountains, probably Namni and Hazzi (= Zaphon = Kasios).[42] These mountains in other texts are in the Storm-god's circle. On a relief at Imamkulu, the Storm-god travels with a wagon, to which are yoked bulls, over three divinized mountains bending under the heavy load--a vivid picture of the god rumbling in thunder across a mountain. The divinized mountains seem to illustrate texts such as the treaty between Mursilis and Duppi-Tessub of Amurru in which the mountains are invoked with other gods as witnesses.[43] Gods are regularly shown in Hittite art standing on mountains. At Yazilikaya, King Tudhaliya IV departed from Hittite custom by having himself in his own lifetime portrayed as a god. He is standing on a mountain.[44]

---

42. On line 19 of a ritual list of mountains and rivers of Bogazköy, *Na-an-ni Ḫa-az-zi* is found among generally north Syrian mountains. Nanni or Namni is not the Amanus, since Am-ma-a-na occurs separately on line 1. The suggestion of H. Th. Bossert in *Orientalia*, 23 (1954), 135f. that Nanni/Namni is Erciyas is unlikely, since presumably Nanni is near Ḫazzi (Zaphon). H. Otten, "Die Berg- und Flusslisten im Hisuwa-Festritual," *ZA*, NS, 25 (1969), 252.

43. *ANET*, p. 205.

44. Ekrem Akurgal, *The Art of the Hittites*, trans. C. McNab (New York: Abrams, 1962), p. 87, and pl. xix.

The memory of a battle with a monster at Hazzi (Zaphon) appears to be preserved, as in Greek and Ugaritic mythology. Teshub and his brother Tashmishu go looking for the stone monster. They are joined by their sister Ishtar. All three ascend Hazzi to find the monster.[45]

It ought to be noted that the Hittite Storm-god, like Syrian Hadad, manifested himself in various locales, including mountains.[46]

In summary, we should expect a lively interchange among Canaanite, Hittite, and Hurrian religions. The mountain did play a significant role in the religions of the area, and these mountains are sometimes explicitly the same mountains that figure in Canaanite religion. At present it is not possible to indicate in any depth the role of the mountain in these religions. It cannot be said whether and in what manner the mountain was cosmic.

---

45. Güterbock, "Hittite Mythology," pp. 168-169.

46. See texts connecting the Weather-god with a number of different places in *PRU*, IV (Paris: Imprimerie Nationale, 1955), 17.27; 17.237. In Ugaritic, seven baals are mentioned in sequence (*CTA* [Paris: Imprimerie Nationale, 1963], 29, 6-11), perhaps Baal-Hadad as he is venerated at different sanctuaries.

II. THE COSMIC MOUNTAIN IN CANAAN

This chapter investigates the cosmic mountain among the peoples in the Syro-Palestinian littoral. In this area mountains are a prominent feature of the landscape, as they are in Anatolia, and entered as obviously into the religious thinking of the people. We extend the term "Canaanite" to include the Northwest Semitic peoples of the area in the second millennium, though it should perhaps be more properly applied to the inhabitants of the Egyptian province Kana'an.

The chapter concentrates almost exclusively in analyzing mythological texts from Ugarit. They are without doubt the best source for understanding Canaanite religion, and it is through them that can be understood the few nonliterary monuments that remain. Although the texts studied are from one city, they represent the religious beliefs of a large area in Syria-Palestine. The geographical areas of the myths include Tyre, Sidon, and Lake Huleh just north of the Sea of Galilee. The Hebrew Bible reveals that elements of the religion of the texts were common even farther south. A comparison of the epics with the prose tablets of Ugarit shows that the language of the epics is a generalized dialect, like that of Homer.[1]

---

1. W. F. Albright, *Yahweh and the Gods of Canaan*

The fact that a different mountain is associated with each deity in the Ugaritic texts provides a natural outline. Each text describing a mountain or a dwelling of a god will be presented, roughly vocalized, then commented upon. When the texts have been analyzed, the little glyptic evidence available will be presented.

El

In his monograph on El which appeared in 1955, Marvin Pope summarized what was then known about the dwelling of El and advanced the discussion by insightful analysis of some of the texts describing El's dwelling.[2] It is possible to go beyond Pope by a more nuanced view of *ḫuršān*, a clearer view of *ḏd*, greater attention to the formal distinctions among the descriptions of El's dwelling, and closer study of the contexts.

On a purely formal basis, we can divide the description of El's dwelling into three types.

Type I

ḥāšuka ʻāṣuka ʻabāṣuka
ʻimmaya paʻnaka talsumāni
ʻimmaya tiwtaḥā ʼišdāka
tôki ḫuršāna [- - - ?]

(Garden City, N.Y.: Doubleday, 1968), pp. 116-118. Moshe Held holds that the epic language as a whole should be considered a kind of "hymnal-epic dialect" like the well-known category in Akkadian literature, *JAOS*, 79 (1959), 175.

2. *El in the Ugaritic Texts*, Supplements to Vetus Testamentum II (Leiden: Brill, 1955), pp. 61-72. Hereafter abbreviated as *EUT*.

[- - ?] ǵūri k-s[3]

Hurry! Hasten! Rush!
To me let your feet run,
To me let your legs hasten,
Toward Mount . . .
. . . mount of k-s.[4]

---

3. The reconstruction of the first tri-colon is based on 3.3.15-17. In reference to El, the above cliché occurs three times (following Herdner's reconstruction); 1.2.1-3; 22-23; 3.10-12. In reference to Baal's mountain, the first tri-colon appears in 3.3.15-17 and 3.4.55-56. The final bi-colon is a composite of 1.2.23; 1.3.11-12, 22. All references are from A. Herdner, *CTA*.

4. A dash is used throughout to indicate a missing letter; ellipsis dots, untranslated texts. *Philological Notes: ḥšk*. This and the two following words, vocalized as infinitives with suffix, are equivalent to imperatives. See C. Brockelmann, *Grundriss der vergleichenden Grammatik der semitischen Sprachen* (Berlin: Reuther & Reichard, 1913), II, 15f; H. L. Ginsberg, *JCS*, 2 (1949), 141f; A. Goetze, *JAOS*, 69 (1949), 181; and M. Pope, *JCS*, 5 (1952), 133-136. *ḥš*. Hebrew *ḥûš*, "to hasten, come quickly." *ʿṣk*. Gordon takes *ḥšk*, *ʿṣk*, and *ʿbṣk* as "Anat's 3 insignia," *Ugaritic Textbook* (Rome: Pontifical Biblical Institute, 1965), 19.907. (Hereafter abbreviated as *UT*.) The context, however, indicates a command of haste, despite the lack of etymology. *ʿbṣ*. Ginsberg suggests as cognate, Arabic *ʾafaṣa*; and Goetze, Akkadian *uppuṣum*; and Pope, Arabic *ʿabaṭa*, "rush headlong," or *ʿaṣaba* (by metathesis), "go quickly, speed along" (in the

The word *ḫršn* demands extended treatment. *Ḫršn* occurs in Ugaritic only twice and each time unfortunately followed by a break in the text, *CTA* 1.2.23; 1.3.22. Marvin Pope has attempted to show "that the Ugaritic *ḫršn* represents essentially the same mythological concept as Akkadian *ḫuršān*, an infernal cosmic mountain (*Weltberg* or *Unterweltberg*), adjacent to the source of the subterranean cosmic waters. The term *ḫršn* thus includes both the mountainous and aqueous features of El's abode and makes it unnecessary to use the words *nhr* and *thm* as elsewhere in usual formula... The nature of El's abode is thus seen to be similar to that of the Sumero-Akkadian Enki-Ea who dwells in the *apsū*."[5] Otto Kaiser has come to essentially the same conclusion regarding the underworld

---

articles cited above). *lsm*. Akkadian *lasāmu*, "to run, gallop." "Knees" can be the subject of *lasāmu* in Akkadian, as in this passage. *twṭḥ*. The word must be parallel to *lsm*, "to run." W. F. Albright corrects the word to *tptṭḥ*, "to me let thy thighs be opened," comparing Akkadian *purīda petū*, in "The Psalm of Habakkuk," *Studies in Old Testament Prophecy*, ed. H. H. Rowley (Edinburgh: T. & T. Clark, 1950), p. 17, n. qq. Possibly *twṭḥ* is the Gt of Arabic *waḥā*, "to hasten"--so Umberto Cassuto, *The Goddess Anath* (Jerusalem: Bialik, 1965), p. 80, and Pope, *JCS*, 5 (1952), 135. However, as Gordon notes, one would expect that the *-wt-* of **tawtaḥā* to assimilate to *-tt-*, as *ʾitrṯ* in *CTA* 3.3.44. Yet note that *yʾitmr* is preserved along with *ytmr* where *ʾit* is assimilated to *-tt-*, *UT*, 19.813.

5. *EUT*, p. 71, and cf. *WM*, I, 281-282.

dwelling of El and his likeness to Enki-Ea in *Die mythische Bedeutung des Meeres in Agypten, Ugarit und Israel*.[6]

Pope's treatment of El's dwelling is in line with his view that El is the deposed king of the gods banished from the supernal mountain of the gods to an infernal haunt.[7] Pope's view of the relation between El and Baal at Ugarit will not be discussed.[8] I wish only to show the extreme unlikelihood of *ḫršn* being an infernal mountain. In the chapter on Mesopotamia, the *Weltberg* or *Unterweltberg* was seen to be based on a misunderstanding of *ḫuršān* and had no foundation in Mesopotamian experience. The texts adduced by Pope on page 70 of his work to prove that *ḫuršān* is an infernal river of judgment can refer equally well to the river ordeal of the upper world.

Ḫršn does of course mean "mountain" in our text, as is shown by its parallelism with *ǵr*, "mountain." "Mountain" is the usual meaning of Akkadian *ḫuršānu* in texts from Boghazköy, Alalakh, and Ugarit, where it is the logogram or determinative for mountain.[9] A recently published Akkadian text from Ugarit helps to explain *ḫršn* in this text. In what appears to be an Akkadian version of the

6. 2nd ed., BZAW, 78 (Berlin: Alfred Töpelmann, 1962), pp. 47-56, esp. p. 55.

7. *EUT*, esp. pp. 92-104.

8. See the judicious remarks of John Gray, *The Legacy of Canaan*, 2nd ed. (Leiden: Brill, 1965), esp. p. 155, and Werner Schmidt, *Königtum Gottes in Ugarit und Israel*, 2nd ed., BZAW, 80 (Berlin: Alfred Töpelmann, 1966), passim, esp. p. 31.

9. *The Assyrian Dictionary* (Chicago: Univ. of Chicago, 1956), *sub voce*.

god-list of *CTA* 29, *^{d}adad be-el huršān ḫa-zi*, "Hadad, the lord of Mount Hazzi (= Zaphon)" (*Ugaritica*, V, 18.4; *RS* 20.24, p. 44), is the equivalent of *bʿl ṣpn*, "Baal Zaphon," of *CTA* 29.5. As with the designation of Baal's mountain, it is probable that *ḫršn* in the El texts was followed by the name of El's mountain. The meaning of *ks* is unknown. Therefore a blank must be left after *ḫuršānu* in the text and the translation "Mount . . ." given.[10]

Types I and II of the descriptions of El's dwelling occur exclusively in what may be called the Baal-Yamm cycle (*CTA* 1 and 2). The Baal-Mot cycle is contained clearly in *CTA* 5 and 6. Though *CTA* 3 and 4 are less certainly typed as belonging to either cycle, they both appear to belong to the Baal-Mot story. In *CTA* 3, *šapšu* is in the hands of Mot in column 5.25-26 and in *CTA* 4.7. 45-54, Mot is the opponent of Baal. *CTA* 4 is sometimes assumed to be in the Yamm cycle because of the mention of *mdd ʾil y* . . . in 2.34 and the fragmentary column 7.1-5 where *mdd. ʾil y* . . . is followed by Baal's changing his

---

10. J. Nougayrol argues tentatively that in 1.18 of the Akkadian god-list, *^{d}ḫuršānu^{MEŠ} u a-mu-tum*, the name of El's mountain is preserved in *amûtu*. There is good reason for Nougayrol to question the usual meaning of *amûtu* as "portent" in this case, yet there is little merit in his suggestion that *ḫuršānu u amûtu* means "mountain and tin." For one thing, *ḫuršānu* is plural, whereas all other mountain names of the gods are in the singular. *Ugaritica*, V (Paris: Imprimerie Nationale, 1968), pp. 52-54.

mind about the window in his palace. The *y* of these fragmentary phrases is assumed to be *y*[*m*]. These two unclear passages are not sufficient evidence for drawing the whole tablet in the Baal-Yamm cycle. *Mdd* is applied not only to Yamm but also to Mot and to *ʾar*[*š*]. It is thus no sure indication of Yamm's presence.

The best indication, however, that *CTA* 1 and 2 belong together as the Baal-Yamm cycle and are distinct from *CTA* 3-6, the Baal-Mot cycle, is the strong resemblance of the Baal-Yamm cycle to the Marduk-Tiamat conflict in *Enūma elīš*. Yamm, like Tiamat, apparently does not rise again after being smitten. Yamm is Tiamat, Sea. Only in the Baal-Yamm cycle does the *pḫr mʿd* play a role, corresponding to the *puḫrum* of the *Enūma elīš*. *Pḫr* does not occur in the Baal-Mot stories. Yamm is given his quietus with magic weapons, as is Tiamat. El's role is shadowy in the Yamm cycle; he is one among the *pḫr ʾilm*, and is given orders by Yamm. He is presumably cowed along with the other gods--a different picture than that of the solitary tent-dweller whose decree is so prized in the Baal-Mot texts. In the Baal-Mot cycle in *CTA* 5, Baal is powerless to resist Mot's command; he descends obediently to the underworld into the power of Mot. In *CTA* 2, however, Baal is the boastful, arrogant warrior, like Marduk in the *puḫrum*, and he finally defeats Yamm. Thorkild Jacobsen has shown the ultimately West Semitic origin of the battle between Marduk and Tiamat in *Enūma elīš* and suggests that the myth was brought to Babylon by the Amorites.[11] I suggest that the Baal-Yamm and the Marduk-

11. "The Battle between Marduk and Tiamat," *JAOS*, 88 (1968), 104-108.

Tiamat conflicts are both reflexes of an originally Canaanite myth. In comparison with the Baal-Yamm cycle, the Baal-Mot cycle seems more seasonal and tied to the agricultural cycle.[12] Types I and II of the description of El and his dwelling are a different type from type III, which is found in the Baal-Mot cycle.[13]

More specifically in this passage, the command to come to the mount of El in 1.2.1-3 and 21-23 is given to Anat. The command to put aside war, to pour peace in the earth, is given to Anat elsewhere only by Baal, in 3.3. 11-17 and 3.4.52-56. Here Baal appears to have won a victory and to be telling Anat on another battlefield to lay down arms and come to the victory celebration. In the Baal text, Anat then goes to El and demands a house for Baal as a recognition of his newly won kingship. El's command in this text must be similar. Anat is to lay down arms in her fight against Yamm because Yamm has been declared winner. This interpretation of 1.2 is supported by 1.3 in which Koshar wa-Khasis is ordered by El to build a house for Yamm to symbolize his rule.

---

12. One should note the alternation between the dry and wet character of Mot's realm. At times it is described as watery and miry and other times as dry, like the infertile steppe. Could there be a mixing of the original domiciles of Yamm and Mot (the god of the unfertile steppe)?

13. The Baal-Mot "type" in 1.2.21-25 combines elements of types I and III which could easily occur, given the techniques of oral composition.

Type II

['iddaka panīma] lā yattinā
tôki ǵūri 'il!i ʻim puḫ!ri môʻidi
'ap 'ilūma laḥā[mu] yaṯibū
banū qudši la-ṯarāmu
baʻlu qamu ʻalê 'ili
halāmu 'ilūma tiphūhumā
tiphūna mal'akê yammi
taʻudatê ṯāpiṭi [nahari]
ta[ǵ]liyū 'il!ūma ra'šātihumū
la-ẓāri barakātihumū
wa-la-kaḥṯi zubūlihumū

(2.1.19-24, paralleled in 13-15)

Then they set face
Toward the Mount of El,
Toward the meeting of the (divine) council.
Then the gods were sitting to eat,
The Holy Ones, to dine.
Baal was standing at El's side.
As soon as the gods saw them,
Saw the messengers of Yamm,
The envoys of Judge River,
The gods dropped their heads
Onto their knees,
Down on their princely thrones.

Several words require comment. The tablet reads *ǵr ll*, "the mount l-l," to which there are no known parallels. We read *ǵr 'il*, "the mount of El." Elsewhere *pḫr mʻd* is paired with *'il* as it is in our text. There are several mistakes in this column, *h* for *ḥ* in line 20 and *h* for *'i* in line 23.[14]

Pḫr is obviously the *puḫrum* of Akkadian, the popular assembly of Mesopotamia and particularly the assembly of *Enūma eliš*.[15] In the Akkadian version of the list of gods in *CTA* 29, *^{d}pu-hur ilani^{MEŠ}*, "the assembly of the gods" (*Ugaritica*, V, 18.18; *RS* 24.20, pp. 44-45), is the equivalent of *phr 'ilm*, "assembly of the gods," of *CTA* 29. rev. 7. In the Baal myths, *pḫr* always means the assembly of the gods under the presidency of El.[16] *Mʿd* is from the root *yʿd*, "to appoint, decide," and only occurs in Ugaritic in the phrase *pḫr mʿd*. The *mʿd* seems to define further the *pḫr*: the meeting of the gods is for

---

14. Otto Kaiser finds that *ǵr ll* (or *ǵr 'i!l*) is not necessarily the dwelling of El, but a place where the Ugaritic gods meet for council, *Die mythische Bedeutung des Meeres*, pp. 54-55. In our view, Kaiser stresses too much the parallel of Enki-Ea to El, neglects *CTA* 1.3.21-24 which presents an authoritative El living on a mountain, and overemphasizes the hostility between El and Baal. On the last point, see the balanced analyses mentioned in n. 8 above.

15. Thorkild Jacobsen, "Primitive Democracy in Mesopotamia," *JNES*, 2 (1943), 159-172, repr. in *TIT*, pp. 157-170.

16. In *CTA* 34.7, *dr 'il wp*[-]*r bʿl* occurs in a list of offerings. Gordon and Herdner restore *p*[*ḫ*]*r*, while Bauer, Dhorme, Dussaud, and Ginsberg restore *p*[*g*]*r* on the basis of 1.12. See Herdner's note at the passage. The evidence is uncertain.

decisions. Hence the appropriateness of "the meeting of the (divine) council."[17]

In the Baal texts, *pḫr* occurs only in the phrases, *pḫr mʿd* and *puḫru banī ʾili-mi*, "the assembly of the sons of El," reflecting the belief that El is the progenitor of all the gods. Other terminology used to describe the divine assembly are *ʿdt ʾilm*, probably to be vocalized and translated as *ʿidatu ʾilīma*, "the assembly of the gods" (15.2.7, 11), and *dr ʾil*, *dāru ʾili*, "the circle of El," *CTA* 15.3.19; 34.7).[18] Only in the Baal-Yamm cycle and the Krt epic among the myth texts does the asembly of El occur.[19]

The assembly of the gods figures prominently in the liturgical texts. We have already mentioned the *pḫr ʾilm*

---

17. The word *mʿd* describes the assembly of eleventh century Byblos, as we learn from the Wen-Amun papyrus. "When morning came, he (Zakar-Baal) had his assembly (*mwʿd*, sing. masc. noun with human rather than land determinative) summoned, and he stood in their midst and said to the Theker, 'Why have you come?'" John A. Wilson, "The Assembly of a Phoenician City," *JNES*, 4 (1945), 245; *ANET*, p. 29.

18. For this meaning of *dr*, see F. Neuberg, "An Unrecognized Meaning of Hebrew *Dôr*," *JNES*, 9 (1950), 215-217, and F. M. Cross, "The Council of Yahweh in Second Isaiah," *JNES*, 12 (1953), 274, n. 1.

19. In an obscure context of 10.1.3-5, *bn ʾil*, "the sons of El," *pḫr ʾilm*, "the assembly of El (or "the gods"), and *dr dt šmm*, "the circle of the heavens," may be in parallel.

of *CTA* 29. rev. 7, a list of deities, and its Akkadian counterpart, *^{d}pu-ḫur ilāni^{MEŠ}*. In another text, sacrifice is said to be offered to the following gods:

yittaši'u la-'abī banī 'ili
yittaši'u la-dāri banī 'ili
la-mipḫarati banī 'ili

(32.17, 34, restored)

It is borne to the father of the sons of El.
It is borne to the circle of the sons of El.
To the assembly, the sons of El.

Other liturgical texts are: *dr ʾil*, "the circle of El" (34.7), *ʾil bn ʾil*, "the gods(s) of the sons of El," *dr bn ʾil*, "the circle of the sons of El," *mpḫrt bn ʾil*, "the assembly of the sons of El" (30.1-3), and *pḫr ʾilm*, "the assembly of the gods" (*Ugaritica*, V 9.9; *RS* 24.143, p. 580).

In post-Ugaritic times, judging from the meager inscriptional evidence, the assembly of the gods continued to be treated as a divine entity alongside of, but not apparently including, the major deities of the locale. In the mid-tenth century at Byblos, the *mpḫrt ʾl gbl*, "the assembly of the gods of Byblos," are invoked after the triad of El, Baal Shamem, and Baalat, to lengthen the days of Yehimilk (*KAI* 4).[20] In the eighth century Karatepe inscription, *bʿl šmm wʾl qn ʾrṣ wšmš ʿlm wkl dr bn ʾlm*, "Baal Shamem, El the Creator of the Earth and the

20. H. Donner and W. Röllig, *Kanaanäische und aramäische Inschriften* (Weisbaden: Harrassowitz, 1966). Hereafter abbreviated as *KAI*.

Eternal Sun and the whole circle of the sons of El," are called upon to protect the inscription (*KAI* 26.3.18-19). In the Arslan Tash inscription of the seventh century, we find *rb dr kl qdšm*, "the great (ones) of the assembly of all the holy ones" (*KAI* 27.12).[21] In the Persian period, "all the gods of Byblos" are invoked in the inscriptions of Shiptibaal (*KAI* 9.B.5-6, uncertain reading) and Yeḥawmilk (*KAI* 10.16, uncertain reading).

In some circles of Canaanite religion, then, the assembly of the gods held an important place. So important a place does it hold in this text that there is a virtual equivalence between El as the head of the assembly and the assembly itself. In 2.1, *pḫr m*ʿ*d* is in parallel with *ǵr* ʾ*il* and to *t̲r* ʾ*ab(y/h)* ʾ*lm* twice.

In the Hebrew Bible, the assembly of the gods appears but plays a diminished role, as might be expected. In Psalm 29, generally recognized as strongly Canaanite, the *bᵉnê* ʾ*ēlîm*, "the sons of the gods," or "the gods," ascribe first place to Yahweh in a heavenly assembly. In Deuteronomy 32, perhaps of the tenth century, "the sons of God" are allotted the nations while Yahweh's portion is his people (vv. 8-9, LXX). In Psalm 82, God prevails in the ʿ*ᵃdat* ʾ*ēl*, "the divine council" *bᵉqereb* ʾ*ᵉlōhîm*, "in the midst of the gods," but condemns the gods because of their unjust judgments. Psalm 82 lets us see the

21. Frank Moore Cross and Richard J. Saley, "Phoenician Inscriptions on a Plaque of the Seventh Century B.C. from Arslan Tash in Upper Syria," *BASOR*, 197 (1970), 42-49, esp. p. 45 and nn. 19 and 21.

process whereby the Canaanite pantheon was reduced in Israel to powerlessness.

Of all the texts mentioned, the Ugaritic text cited above, type II, gives the clearest picture of the divine council. The assembly sits on the mountain. Their deliberations are preceded, as in the Mesopotamian *puḫrum*, by eating and drinking. The assembly receives the messengers of Yamm who demand that Baal, the young god waiting upon El, be given up. El, despite Baal's vigorous defense, acquiesces. Evidently, the assembly, with El, is being asked to ascribe kingship to Yamm, a function of the *bᵉnê ʾēlîm* in Psalm 29. Functions of the divine assembly hinted at in the Hebrew Bible are lordship of the nations (Deut. 32:8-9), acclaiming the king of the gods (Ps. 29), and judging in a court of law (Ps. 82). Only the acclaiming of the king is depicted in *CTA* 2.1.

The position of El is important. Though presumably frightened together with the other gods, as he is frightened before Anat in *CTA* 3.5, he is virtually equivalent to the whole assembly. In *CTA* 2.1, the *pḫr mʿd* is parallel to *ǵr ʾil* and to *ṯr ʾab(y/h) ʾil* twice.

El is in the midst of his assembly, a picture similar to the Mesopotamian *puḫrum*. The assembly meets on a mountain which seems West Semitic rather than East Semitic. He is not the forceful lone patriarch, living in a tent, as in type III. Here he is frightened. He speaks with authority (*ṭhm*), but only to hand over Baal in obedience to Yamm. In *CTA* 2.4, Baal takes matters into his own hands. With the help of two magic clubs made for him by Koshar wa-Khasis, Baal eliminates Yamm.

In type III, El's *ṯḥm* makes a king and in *CTA* 6.1, El, almost casually, decides who may be a candidate for Baal's position. Here, Baal is forced to fight for himself.

Type III

There are two versions of type III, or more accurately, the anomalous second version (b) seems to be a conflate of types I and III, probably owing to oral composition. The Hittite version, like other Hittite reflections of Canaanite myth, is no longer couched in Canaanite poetic form. It resembles type III.

a) ʼiddaka lā tattinā panīma
ʻim ʼili mabbikī naharêmi
qirba ʼapīqī tihām(ā)têmi
tagliyā ḏadī ʼili wa-tabāʼā
qarašī malki ʼabī šanīma

(3.5.13-16; 4.4.20-24; 6.1.32-36; 2.3(?).4-5; 17.6.46-49. The conjugation has arbitrarily been made dual).

Then they set face
Toward El at the sources of the Two Rivers,
In the midst of the pools of the Double-Deep.
They entered the tent(s) of El and went into
The tent-shrine of the King, Father of Years

b) ʼiddaka lā yatti[nu panīma
ʻim luṭpāna] ʼili dū pāʼidi
tôki ḫuršāna . . .
yagliyu ḏadī ʼili wa-yabāʼu
qarašī malki ʼabī šanīma

(1.3.21-24)

Then he set face
Toward the Benign One, El the Compassionate,
In the midst of Mount . . .
He entered the tent of El and went into
The tent-shrine of the king, Father of Years.

c) na-aš ŠA ^{íd}Ma-a-la ḫar-šum-na-aš a-ar-[aš]
na-aš A-NA] ^{d}EL-ku-ni-ir-ša ŠA ^{d}A-še-er-tu$_4$
^{lú}MU-DI-ŠU a-ar-[aš na-aš-kan ŠA] ^{d}El-ku-ni-ir-ša
^{giš}ZA.LAM.GAR-aš an-da pa-it

He went his way and betook himself to the well-spring of the Mala-River. He came to El-Kunirsha, the husband of Ashertu, and entered El-Kunirsha's tent.[22]

Several words in the text require comment.[23] For *ʾapq*, archaic Hebrew poetry suggests both "channels" (Job 6.15) and "pools" (2 Sam. 22:16 = Ps. 18:18). A new text, *ʾil mbk nhrm bʿdt thmt*, "El at the sources of the Two Rivers, at the meeting place (?) of the Double-Deep" (*Ugaritica*, V, 7.3; *RS* 24.244, p. 564), substituting *ʿdt* for *ʾapq*, suggests that *ʾapq* is the area where the sea and the river meet.

Marvin Pope has assembled the evidence that the abode of El was localized at Aphaca, modern Khirbet Afqa in Syria, the impressive site where the Nahr Ibrahim

---

22. Translation of Albrecht Goetze, *ANET*, p. 519. For Hittite text, see H. Otten, *MIO*, 1 (1953), 125-150, and *Revue Hittite et Asianique*, 26 (1968), 26.

23. For the entire passage, consult M. Pope, *EUT*, pp. 61-81, and F. M. Cross, *HTR*, 55 (1962), 249-250.

seems to rise out of a huge cave. Even though El's abode was localized in Syria by the Ugaritians, it had a mythical, nongeographical character. Pope sees *mkb nhrm*, "the sources of the Two-Rivers," and *ʾapq thmt*, "the pools of the Double-Deep," as evidence that "El resides in aqueous and subterranean environs," the place of the subterranean waters, and places El's abode in the underworld, El having been deposed. He is in the underworld using the likes of Mot and Yamm to regain his throne.[24]

Mbk[25] *nhrm* and *ʾapq thmtm* are not in the underworld. As W. F. Albright and others have noted, the terms are not to be separated from Sumerian *íd-ka-min-ne*, Akkadian *pî nârâti* (*kilallê*), "the mouth of the (two) rivers."[26] S. N. Kramer has now gathered the evidence which shows that the mouth or source of the two rivers (= Tigris and Euphrates) is the Persian Gulf. The ancient Sumerian priests and poets conceived the debouchment of the Tigris and the Euphrates as the mouth which "drank" the Persian Gulf. In their poetic view, the sea fed the rivers, not the mountains of Armenia.[27] The language in the passage,

---

24. *EUT*, pp. 92-104.

25. For a study of the root **nbk/npk*, see G. M. Landes, "The Fountain of Jazer," *BASOR*, 144 (1956), 31-34.

26. W. F. Albright, *Archaeology and the Religion of Israel*, 3rd ed. (Baltimore: The Johns Hopkins Press, 1953), pp. 72, 194. Albright was mistaken, however, in locating "the mouth of the rivers" in the mountains of Armenia.

27. "Dilmun, the Land of the Living," *BASOR*, 96 (1944), 28, n. 41.

then, is borrowed from old Mesopotamian poetry which places the god in paradise, the source of life-giving waters.[28] These waters are not in the underworld. The underworld in the Ugaritic texts is either a sterile steppe or a miry bog. The waters of El's rivers are, on the contrary, life-giving.[29] El lives on the mountain which is described with ancient paradisiacal motifs. In the clear descriptions available of the underworld, Mot's domain, there are no mountains. One enters through the base of mountains but no mountains are mentioned in the underworld.

I have taken *ḏd* as plural, which is frequent in housing terms. Although I have found no extra-Ugaritic cognates for "tent," intra-Ugaritic evidence appears strong for this meaning, and not for "mountain," or "land area." *Ḏd* appears six times in the cliché for El's dwelling (1.3.23; 2.3.5; 3.5.15; 4.4.23; 6.1.34; 17.6.48). In only one of these six passages does a clear word for "mountain," *ḫuršānu*, appear with which *ḏd* might possibly

---

28. Eden is the source of life-giving waters in Gen. 2, and the mountain of God is the source in Ezek. 47:1-12, Zech. 13:8, and Joel 4:18 (E. VV. 3.18).

29. Mrs. E. Douglas Van Buren in *The Flowing Vase and the God with Streams of Water* (Berlin: H. Schoetz, 1933) has shown that the vase and the streams of water issuing from it were symbols "of the perpetually recurring streams of living water productive of the fruitfulness and abundance bestowed by divine munificence," quoted in her *Symbols of the Gods in Mesopotamian Art* (Rome: Pontifical Biblical Institute, 1945), pp. 124-125.

be in parallel, 1.3.23. In this passage, "b" above, the final bi-colon with *ḏd* appears to be intrusive. In the other four uses in the descriptions of El's dwelling, there is no mention of a mountain. The description of El's abode otherwise makes use of a rigid parallelism: *mabbikū // ʾapīqū; naharāmi // tihāmātāmi; ʾilu // milku ʾabū šanīma; tagliyu // tabāʾu*. It would be expected therefore that *ḏd* would be in parallel to *qarašū*, "tent-frame, tent." *Ḏd* as "tent" is made more certain by the use of *gly* to describe the mode of access to *ḏd*. In the Hebrew Bible, *gly* is used of an uncovering or rolling back. It is highly appropriate to describe entering a tent by "rolling back the tent flap."[30] In the only instance of *gly* outside of our El cliché, it is used to mean "to enter (a domicile)," and is there also in parallel with *bāʾu*, 16.4.4.

Is there any evidence outside of the parallelism in the El cliché that *ḏd* means "tent?" *CTA* 19.211-214 gives us clear evidence.[31]

maǵaya[t] Paǵatu la-’ahalīma
rigmu la-Yaṭ[pāna yû]bal
’aguratunu ba’at la-ḏadīka
[Paǵatu] ba’at ba-⟨’a⟩halīma

Pagat has reached the tent
Word was brought to Yatpan.
"Our hired woman is at thy tent,
Pagat is in the tent."

30. Suggestion of Conrad L'Heureux.

31. The occurrences of *ḏd* in 3.5.17; 19.220; and 18.4.15 are unfortunately too obscure to help.

Ḏd in this text parallels *ʾahlm*. On intra-Ugaritic evidence, then, it seems likely that *ḏd* means "tent," or part of a tent.[32]

---

32. F. M. Cross has argued that though *ḏ* has shifted to *d* except in archaizing texts, there are a few words in which the grapheme *ḏ* represents not only /*ḏ*/, its original value, but also /*ṯ*/. Thus *ḏd*, "breast," represents *ṯadu*; *ḏbl*, a place name, is Amarna *šabilu*, biblical *šôbal*, Ugaritic (place name) *ša-bi-il* (?), North Arabic *ṯbl*; *ḏrt*, "vision," is *ṯrt*, Hebrew *šwr*, "to see," Amarna *širtu*, and *ḏd* represents *ṯd*, "mountain" (*HTR*, 55 [1962], 249-250). The assumption behind the equivalence is that *ḏd* means "mountain," and the aim is to prove that "mountain" stands behind the patriarchal title El Shadday.

There are difficulties in some of the words that have been selected. *Ḏd*, "breast": the Ugaritic variety of *ṯd* (4x) and *ḏd* (1x) is reflected in the Hebrew Bible with *dad*, *zîz*, and **šd*, which makes precise derivation difficult. *Ḏbl*, place name in 68.A.7.B.7. Although the left edge of the plates are not clear, Herdner draws  for the first letter in A.7 and  for the first letter in B.7. For this anomalous letter-shape, Virolleaud reads *ǵ* and Gordon reads *ḏ*. Miss Herdner rightly reads an uncertain *ṯ*. Thus the identification with Amarna *šabilu* could stand without proving that /*ṯ*/ stands behind *ḏ*. See also Jonas C. Greenfield, "Amurrite, Ugaritic and Canaanite," *Proceedings of the International Conference on Semitic Studies* (Jerusalem: Israel Academy of Sciences and Humanities, 1969), p. 95.

That El lives in a tent should occasion no surprise. In the Hittite fragment cited above, he lives in a tent. In the Krt epic, the gods live in *ʾahlm* "tents" and *mšknt*, "tabernacles" (15.3.18-19).[33] In the Baal cycle, El's domicile is nowhere certainly called a *bt*, "house," or *hkl*, "temple/palace." The two terms are used of Baal's home (and for Yamm's in *CTA* 1 and 2). El's dwelling is referred to as *mṯb*, "dwelling," and *mẓll*, "shelter," and of course *qrš* "tent-frame," and *ḏd*, "tent." In *CTA* 21, El does indeed have a *bt* and a *hklm*, and in the Aqht legend, both Baal and El have a *bt*. But these are outside the Baal cycle proper (*CTA* 1-11). Within that cycle, El lives in a tent, and the center of interest is Baal's temple.

In the Hittite version, the Storm-god comes to El at the Mala River (= Euphrates)[34] to tell him that Ashertu, the wife of El, has made overtures to him. The struggle for kingly power seems to be behind the episode, especially since in the Old Testament Asherah has become Baal's consort.[35]

---

34. The identification is confirmed by two tablets found at Boghazköy in 1957, in which Akkadian *Purattu* = Hittite *Mala*. John Garstang and O. R. Gurney, *The Geography of the Hittite Empire* (London: British Institute of Archaeology of Ankara, 1959), p. 49.

35. There is no foundation for Pope's assertion that El here is not in his regular dwelling and that he is living away from spouse and house (*EUT*, p. 66). In *CTA* 4, Asherah is also away from El without being estranged from him.

The chief difference between types II and III is the place of El on the mountain. Here he is found alone--there is no mention of other gods--and the gods come to him seeking, not demanding, permissions relating to kingship (except in the Aqhat legend). Even when Asherah with wifely blandishments and Anat with the threat of violence come to El, their very disrespect for El sets in relief the objective power of El's decision, the *ṭḥm*. In type II, El is in the midst of the *pḫr mʿd* and indeed is put in some sort of parallel with them. The mountain character of the assembly of the divine council is there more emphasized. El presumably is cowed along with the other gods at the message of Yamm.

The context of all the texts in the Baal cycle is the building of a palace connected with kingship--for Yamm in 2.3.4-6 and for Baal in 3.5.13-19, 4.4.20-27. In 6.1.32-38, Anat goes to El, evidently to be an onlooker while a substitute king is proclaimed. In the Aqhat legend, 17.6.46-51, the kingship is not involved; Anat merely wants revenge on Aqhat. In the Hittite version, the context is the report of marital infidelity, though possibly with overtones of kingly power.

In those passages dealing with kingship, El's decree plays a large part. The message or decree of El (*ṭḥm*) deserves study to clarify El's activity on his mountain. The decision of El is frequently expressed in the word *ṭḥm*. In epistolary usage which reflects the language of the later stage of Ugarit, the word means the contents of the letter which follows. The message can be of the king, high official, or private citizen. Orders are frequently given in these letters, and the authority of the *ṭhm* is obviously commensurate with the authority of the sender. The myth texts, with the exception of 3.5.38-41 and 4.4.41-44, always reflect preliterary usage when messengers took the place of letters between important personages. The human messengers in place of letters on clay tablets hark back to heroic times. The messengers repeat messages verbatim, as do the clay tablets which replaced them. *Ṭhm* is always in the context of messengers except in the two passages about to be discussed.

The authority inherent in *ṭhm* in the myths seems to vary according to the authority of the sender. The *ṭhm* of Yamm in 2.1. intimidates the assembly of the gods and El, but not Baal. Yet Baal must obey the *ṭhm* of Mot in 5.1 and 2.

A further development beyond the epistolary usage is shown in the parallel passages 3.5.38-41 and 4.4.41-44. In the first, Anat threatenes El with violence if he does not allow Baal's house to be built. In the second, Asherah uses uxorious wiles to the same aim. Both goddesses say:

> taḥumuka ʼilu ḥakima
> ḥukmuka ʻim ʻālami
> ḥayyatu ḥiẓẓati taḥumuka
> malkunu ʼalʼiyānu baʻlu
> ṯāpiṭunu wa-ʼêna dū ʻalênnuhu

> Thy Decree, O El, is wise,
> Thy wisdom lasts forever.
> A life of good fortune is thy command.
> Our king is Aliyan Baal,

Our judge, above whom there is no other.[36]

Here the authority of the epistolary usage has developed into something akin to a hypostasis. El's decree is treated as something almost distinct from him. Note the contrast between the goddesses' assaults on El's person and their esteem of El's decree. No temple is built without El's decree! The development appears reflected in the proper name *ʾltḥm*. One should compare hypostatizations in Mesopotamian and in later Hebrew traditions, particularly the "name" theology, the *dābār* and the *memrāʾ* theology of postbiblical times. El's mountain is a place of power--a power of decree!

Baal

Baal's mountain, *ṣpn*, occurs in extra-Ugaritic occurrences as well as in the Ugaritic corpus. Therefore an occasional look outside the Ugaritic texts is important.

The vocalization of *ṣpn* in Ugaritic on the basis of later Hebrew *ṣāpôn* may have been *ṣapānu*. In no case in Ugaritic does it mean simply "north," its usual meaning in the Bible. *Ṣpn* is best derived from *ṣpy*, "to look out, spy out" (in formation corresponding to *ḥāzôn* from *ḥzy*), not *ṣpn*, "to hide, to treasure up." The usual biblical meaning "north" is secondary. Since the mountain Zaphon was north of Palestine, the direction north was derived from the name of the mountain, as the direction

36. The translation follows Albright's in "Baal-Zephon," *Festschrift Alfred Bertholet* (Tübingen: J. C. B. Mohr, 1950), p. 5, n. 3.

west was derived from *yam*, "sea," and "south," from *negeb*, "dry land."[37]

In Ugaritic, *ṣpn* can have four meanings: (1) the mountain today called Jebel ʾel-Aqraʿ, about 50 km north of Ras Shamra at the mouth of the Orontes; (2) the mountain dwelling of the god Baal, especially in the mythic texts; (3) the deified mountain *ṣpn*, especially in the liturgical texts and in proper names; (4) part of the epithet *Bʿl ṣpn* (never in the mythic texts and frequently in extra-Ugaritic texts).

Ṣpn as Jebel ʾel-Aqraʿ. That *ṣpn* designates an earthly locale is seen in the list of towns in 71.50, *ḫlb ṣpn* "(the town of) Halbu of *ṣpn*," and the equation: *āl Ḫalbi ḪUR.SAG Ha-zi(ši) = Ḫlb ṣpn*. The town of Halbu of Mount Hazzi = Halbu of Zaphon.[38] *Ṣpn* was thus the Canaanite name of the mountain called Ḫazzi in Akkadian and the Hittite treaties. Early Greek *Kasios* is the phonetic equivalent of Hittite *Ḫazzi*.[39]

Ṣpn as the mountain dwelling of Baal. That *ṣpn* is a mountain dwelling is shown by *mrym* (probably a miqtal formation from the root *rw/ym*, "to be high," so "heights"), by the fact that one must ascend *(ʿly)* it and by the term

37. Pope, *WM*, I, 258.

38. Charles Virolleaud, "Les Villes et les corporations de royaume d'Ugarit," *Syria*, 21 (1940), 123-151, and W. F. Albright, "Baal-Zephon," p. 2.

39. A. Goetze, "The City Khalbi and the Khapiru People," *BASOR*, 79 (1940), 33, and W. F. Albright, "Baal-Zephon," p. 2 and n. 4.

ǵr and *gb*ʿ used to describe it. Here Baal, dead at the hands of Mot, is buried and mourned by Anat (6.1.14-31).

Ṣpn is where Baal and Mot, like two animals, fight until Shapshu frightens Mot away by threatening him with El's wrath (6.6.12-34). From a speech of Anat, we learn that *ṣpn* is the scene of another furious combat. On one occasion, she is provoked to describe her past battles for Baal against the monsters. "Did I not crush the beloved of El, Yamm? Did I not destroy El's stream, Rabbim? Did I not muzzle the dragon?" Among the monsters

> ʼimtaḫiṣ kaspa ʼittariṯ ḫarūṣa
> ṭāridi baʿla ba-miryami ṣapāni
> m š ṣ ṣ . (?) kʿ(ṣ/l) (?) ʼudnāhu
> gārišihu la-kissiʼi mulkihu
> la-n-ḫati la-kaḥṯi darkatihu
> (3.3.43-4.47)

> Did I not wrest the silver, plunder the gold
> Of the one(s) who would drive Baal from the heights of Zaphon,
> . . . . .
> Of the one(s) who would expel him from his royal throne,
> From the dais, from his powerful seat?

It is likely that the battle between Mot and Baal already referred to, and this battle, are related. Baal must win his kingship over a multitude of enemies.

Elsewhere (5.1.1-8), Baal slays the same monsters whom Anat claims to have killed in the passage above. In a fragmentary text described by Albright as "part of an incantation,"[40] a battle between Anat and the dragon is related.

ba-'arṣi m-ḫ-n-m ṯarapa yamma
lašānāmi tilḥakā šamīma
tatrupā yamma ḏanabatāmi
tunn!āna lā-šabūma tašītu
tirkasu lā-miryami laban[āni

(*PRU*, II, 3.8-10)

In the land of Mḫnm he (the dragon) swirled the sea,
His double tongue licked the heavens,
His twin tails churned up (?) the sea.
She fixed the unmuzzled dragon.
She bound (him) to the heights of Lebanon.

Instead of Zaphon, the battle appears to be taking place on Lebanon. The transfer of the mountain of battle from Zaphon to Lebanon is not surprising given the fluidity of Canaanite myth and the fact that by the thirteenth century a small hill in the Nile Delta had come to be called Zaphon (Exod. 14:2, 9) and apparently was the repository of a story of conflict with dragons (Herodotus III.5). In Hittite myth, Hazzi (Zaphon), is also the scene of strife with monsters. In Greek myth, Zeus (= Baal) fights with Typhon and other monsters on his holy mountain Kasios (= Zaphon). In *CTA* 1.5, an obscure passage, Baal fights on Zaphon. In *PRU*, II, 1, Baal slays the dragon.

On Zaphon, Koshar wa-Khasis builds a huge palace for Baal, after El has given his permission.

---

40. *BASOR*, 150 (1957), 36-37, n. 5.

ḥūša turmamūna hēkalūma
ba-tôk ṣ r r t ṣapāni
ʼalpa šadi ʼaḫada bêtu
rabbata kumani hēkalu
(4.5.116-119)

Hurry! Let a palace be raised
In the midst of *ṣrrt* Zaphon!
Let the house cover a thousand acres,
Ten thousand hectares, the palace!

To Baal on his mountain are brought many messages, the command of Mot to descend to the underworld as a captive (5.1.10-2.19), the news of El's permission for Baal's palace (4.5.84-85), and the announcement that young nobles (buffalo and wild ox) have been born to Baal (10.3.28-37). In the latter two messages, Anat is the messenger and the verb used is *bšr* "to proclaim good news."

Zaphon is the scene of frequent banqueting. Baal fetes Koshar wa-Khasis before the latter sets to work on his palace (4.5.106-110); a victory banquet appears to be described in 3.1.1-22. Baal gives a great dedicatory feast to the seventy gods when his temple is finished (4.6.38-59). In a recently published text, Baal is seated on his holy mountain Zaphon. On the verso, Anat washes her hands, takes a lyre, and sings. Although eating and drinking are not mentioned, the scene has the appearance of a feast (*Ugaritica*, V, 3; *RS* 24.245, pp. 557-558).

Ṣpn as deified mountain. Among the liturgical texts (rubrics and lists of offerings) of Ras Shamra, the deified mountain *ṣpn* occurs frequently. A typical example is *l ṣpn gdlt*, "a large animal to (the god) Zaphon."

That Zaphon is the deified mountain, and not a shortened form of Baal Zaphon is shown clearly in *Ugaritica*, V, 13. 9-10 (*RS* 24.253, p. 592), *š l bʿl ṣpn dqt l ṣpn*, "a sheep for Baal Zaphon and a *dqt* 'small cattle' for Zaphon." In *Ugaritica*, V, 9.6 (*RS* 24.643, p. 580), *ǵrm*, "mountains," receive the same sacrificial offerings as the gods other than El and Baal, one sheep. In the same volume, among the Akkadian texts, in 18.18 (*RS* 20.24, p. 45) is found *ᵈḫuršānu u a-mu-tu*[*m*, with the sign of divinity before the Akkadian word for mountains (*ḫuršānu*). It appears to be the deified mountain who appears in the proper name *ʿpṣpn* (*PRU*, V, 85.9) and in the name from the seventh century Assur Ostrakon, *grṣpn*, *gerṣapun*, "The Protected One of Zaphon." Compare also the Akkadian name *Gír-ṣa-pu-na* (*KAI* 233.3).[41]

The deified mountain is well known from Hittite and Hurrian mythology. Hazzi, the Hittite and Hurrian equivalent for Zaphon, is often paired with the mountain Namni/ Nanni as satellites of the Storm-god and in treaties.

In the mythological texts, Zaphon as a deified mountain appears in 16.1.6-9 (= 16.2.106-109).[42] Ginsberg's

---

41. In late Phoenician times the god occurs in the names *ṣpnṣdq* (Pope, *JBL*, 85 [1966], 481), *ʾyṣpn* (*KAI* 159.5) from Henschir Medeina, and *ṣpnbʿl*, "Zaphon is Lord," or "May Baal protect" (*KAI* 93.1) from Carthage. See Frauke Gröndahl, *Die Personennamen der Texte aus Ugarit* (Rome: Pontifical Biblical Institute, 1967), pp. 111, 189.

42. I disagree with Albright who understands *ṣpn* here as Baal Zaphon, in "Baal-Zephon," p. 3, n. 4. He

translation in *ANET* (p. 147) is followed:

tabkiyuka 'abī ĝūru ba'li
ṣapānu ḥēlu-mi qudši
'anāyu ḥēlu-mi 'aduru
ḥēlu raḥābu miknapati

The mountain of Baal weeps for you, my father,
Zaphon, the holy circuit.
The mighty circuit weeps,
The circuit broad of span.

The enigmatic phrase *'il ṣpn* occurs three times in Ugarit, 3.3.26; 29.1; and *Ugaritica*, V, 3.3. (*RS* 24.245, p. 557). In *CTA* 29, a list of deities, *'il ṣpn* appears at the head of the list before *'il 'ib*, *dgn*, *b'l ṣpn* and other gods. In the Akkadian equivalent of this list in *Ugaritica*, V, 18 (*RS* 20.24, pp. 44-45), there is no equivalent to *'il ṣpn*, although the other gods have their Akkadian counterparts. In the myth text, 3.3.26, the best translation of *'ibĝayuhu ba-tôk ĝūriya 'ili ṣapāni ba-qudši ba-ĝūri naḥlatiya* is "I will seek it in the midst of my mountain, divine Zaphon in the shrine, in the mount of my heritage."[43] In *Ugaritica*, V, 3.3 (*RS*

---

translates, "The women will chant, O my father,/The co-wives will mourn thee, my father!/'O mountain, Baal-Zaphon, O holy phoenix./O bark, "Glorious Phoenix,"/Phoenix wide of wings!'" The cola beginning "O mountain" is the beginning of a dirge which the wailing women will sing. In *Ugaritica*, V, 13.25 (*RS* 24.253, p. 592) occurs the phrase *'nt ḥl*.

43. Other translators have understood El Zaphon as

24.2.45, p. 557) *ʾil ṣpn* occurs; *ba-tôki ǵūrihu ʾili ṣapāni*, "in the midst of his mountain, divine Zaphon."

Ṣpn in the divine name Baal Zaphon. In the non-mythological texts, reference to the deity Baal Zaphon occurs ten times. Most occurrences are in lists of sacrifices which stipulate a certain sacrifice to be offered to Baal Zaphon. Very little can be learned about the nature of the god, apart from the fact that he always appears in the lists after El. Two instances, however, are instructive. In *PRU*, II, 18, a letter from the king of Ugarit to the king of Egypt, one should read with Otto Eissfeldt,[44] *la-panê baʿli ṣapani baʿliya*, "before Baal-Zaphon, my lord," said by the king of Ugarit. It is in loose parallel to *la-panī Amun wa-la-panī ʾilī miṣrêmi*, "before Amun and before the gods of Egypt." Here Baal-Zaphon seems to be the national god of the city of Ugarit, just as Amon seems to be the chief god of the Egyptian panthion, at least for the reigning Pharaoh. In *Ugaritica*, V, 9.4-6 (*RS* 24.643, p. 580) is found *bʿl ḫlb ʾalp w š/bʿl ṣpn ʾalp w š/ṯrṯy ʾalp w š*, "Baal Halbu, ox and sheep/Baal Zaphon, ox and sheep/Ṯrṯy, ox and sheep."

---

the name of the mountain. Dahood offers "in the midst of my towering mountain Zaphon," comparing Ps. 36:7 *harᵉre ʾēl*. *Ugaritic-Hebrew Philology* (Rome: Pontifical Biblical Institute, 1965), p. 15. Cf. also the note of J. Nougayrol in *Ugaritica*, V, pp. 50-51.

44. Eissfeldt, "Baʿal Ṣaphon von Ugarit und Amon von Ägypten," *FF*, 36 (1962), 338-340, repr. in *Kleine Schriften*, IV (Tübingen: J. C. B. Mohr, 1968), 53-57. (Hereafter abbreviated as *KS*.)

In this list of divinities, the three gods mentioned get an ox and a sheep in contrast to the other gods (including *ʾil ʾib* and *ʾil* who get only a sheep). Baal is here represented as connected to two different locales, the city of Halbu and the mountain of Zaphon. In the list of deities, 29.6-11, *bʿlm* is repeated six times in a row after *bʿl ṣpn*. The Akkadian version of the list in *Ugaritica*, V, 18 (*RS* 20.24, p. 45), has, after *dAdad be-el ḫuršān ḫa-zi* in 1.4 (corresponding to *bʿl ṣpn* of *CTA* 29. 5), *dAdad II*, *dAdad III* up to *dAdad VII*. Probably these are baals of local sanctuaries.

In *Ugaritica*, V, 13.13-14, 17 (*RS* 24.253, p. 592), a liturgical text, sacrifice is listed for *ʿnt ṣpn*! As has been shown, in the mythological tests there is a close relation of Anat to Zaphon especially in its defense. Charles Virolleaud's reading of *PRU*, II, 4.21, *ʾilt ṣpn* where the goddess would be Anat, should be noted.

In 1932, Eissfeldt listed all the occurrences of Baal Zaphon then available. In 1950, Albright was able to extend and correct what Eissfeldt had provided[45] and to show more precisely the god's relation to Egypt. Baal Zaphon will be discussed further in the next chapter.

The texts describing Baal's dwelling are less easily typed than those describing El's. None of them occurs in the Baal-Yamm cycle (*CTA* 1 and 2), though six occur in *CTA* 3 and the early columns of *CTA* 4 which are less clearly identified as being part of the Baal-Mot cycle.

---

45. Eissfeldt, *Baal Zaphon, Zeus Casios und der Durchzug der Israeliten durchs Meer* (Halle: Niemeyer, 1932). Albright, "Baal-Zephon," pp. 1-14.

Three of the formal types of descriptions follow here.

Type I

ʾiddaka lā yattinā panīma
ʿim baʿli miryami ṣapāni

(3.4.81-82; 4.5.84-85; 5.1.10-11)

Then they set face
Toward Baal (on) the heights of Zaphon.

In 3.4.81-82, Anat goes to the heights of Zaphon in answer to Baal's summons to hear an important revelation. The exact nature of Baal's revelation is not completely clear, but apparently it is that the harmony of nature is restored and that life-giving rains will return to the earth (3.3.17-28). Anat is to cease from the spectacular carnage that is described in column two and is to go to Baal on the mountain. When she arrives, Baal dismisses his wives and sets a feast for Anat. The text then breaks off.

In 4.5.84-85, Anat announces to Baal the glad tidings that El has granted permission to build his palace through Asherah's intercession.

In 5.1.10-11, the servants of Baal go to Zaphon to relay to Baal the command (*tḥm*) of Mot that Baal is to go into the underworld. Baal is then stricken with fear.

Type II

la-dôdi ʾalʾiyāni baʿli
yiddi pidrayyi bitti ʾāri
ʾahbati ṭallayyi bitti rabbi
dôdi ʾarṣayyi bitti y-ʿ-b-d-r
kī-mā ǵalmāmi wa-ʿurubāni
la-paʿnê ʿanati huburā wa-qullā

tištaḥwiyā kabbidā hiyata
wa-rugumā la-batūlati ʻanati
ṯanniyā la-yab!imati l-ʼumi
taḥumu ʼalʼiyāni baʻli
hawatu ʼalʼiyu qarrādīma
q-r-y-y- ba-ʼarṣi milhamata (?)
šītī ba-ʻaparīma dôdaya-mi (?)
sakī šalāma la-kabidi ʼarṣi
ʼaribī dôda la-kabidi šadīma
ḥāšuka ʻāṣuka ʻabāṣuka
ʻimmaya paʻnāka talsumāni
ʻimmaya tiwtaḥā ʼišdāka
d-m rigmu ʼêṯa liya wa-ʼargumaka
hawatu wa-ʼaṯanniyaka
rigmu ʻiṣṣi wa-l-ḫ-šatu ʼabni
t-ʼanaṯu šamīma ʻimma ʼarṣi
tihāmatu ʻimma-n- kabkabīma
ʼabīnu baraqa dū lā tidaʻū šamūma
rigmu lā tidaʻū našūma
wa-lā tabīnu hamultu ʼarṣi
ʼati-mi wa-ʼanāku ʼibǵayuhu
ba-tôki ǵūriya ʼili ṣapāni
baqudši ba-ǵūri naḥlatiya
ba-naʻami ba-gibʻi talʼiyati

(3.3.2-28)

For the love of Aliyan Baal,
The love of Misty One, Daughter of Bright Cloud,
The love of Dewy One, Daugher of Showers,
The love of Earthie, Daughter of Yʻbdr.
So then, O lads, enter.
At the feet of Anat bow and fall down,

Worship and honor her.
And say to the Maiden Anat,
Repeat to the Bride of the People.
"Message of Aliyan Baal,
The word of the Conqueror of the Heroes.
Remove (?) war from the earth,
Set love in the dust. (?)
Pour out peace in the depths of the earth,
Make love increase (?) in the depths of the fields.
Hurry! Hasten! Run!
To me let your feet run,
To me let your legs hasten.
For (?) I have a speech and I will speak it,
A message and I will repeat it.
The speech of wood and the whisper of stone,
The converse (?) of heaven with the earth,
Of the deeps with the stars.
I understand lightning which the heavens do not know,
Speech which men do not know,
And the multitude of the earth do not understand.
Come, and I will seek it,
In the midst of my mountain, divine Zaphon,
In the holy place, the mountain of my heritage,
In the chosen spot, on the hill of victory.[46]

---

46. *Philological notes:* *qryy* . . . *šdm*. For justification of the translation we have tentatively adopted, see A. Goetze, "Peace on Earth," *BASOR*, 93 (1944), 17-20. Difficulties remain, however.

rgm *ʿṣ* *wlḫšt* *ʾabn*. The phrase is puzzling in the extreme, but is best taken as the first third of the

The two terms *nḥlty* and *tl'yt* require comment. The Ugaritic noun *nḥlt* occurs only in the phrases *ǵr nḥlty*,

---

following tri-colon. Metrically: *d-m rigmu 'ê<u>t</u>a; wa-argumuka hawata; wa-'a<u>t</u>anniyuka rigma.* It is also possible to take *'abn* as "I will understand," or "I will reveal," with the second member of the bi-colon.

t'ant šmm ʿm 'arṣ. We take this phrase in some kind of parallelism to *rgm ʿṣ wlḫšt 'abn*, so perhaps "converse," related to Hebrew *'anāh*, "to groan." As will be argued below in detail, the context of both this passage and the parallel passage in 1.3.10-16 is the building of a palace, either for Yamm or for Baal. The palace symbolizes kingship, the office which mediates fertility and cosmic harmony. It is not unreasonable to associate the new possibilities for reconciliation between heaven and earth with the temple on the mountain.

'abn brq. "I will create lightning," John Gray, *Legacy of Canaan*, p. 46, and also G. R. Driver, *CML* (Edinburgh: T. & T. Clark, 1956), p. 89; "thunderbolt (?)," Ginsberg, *ANET*, p. 136; "stones of fire," or the like; Cassuto, *The Goddess Anath*, p. 81; and Pope, *EUT*, pp. 99-100. Fortunately, the formal structure offers us a way out of the puzzle. *'abn* is part of a scheme: *'abn* : *ltdʿ* :: *ltdʿ* : *ltbn*. It is therefore from the root *byn*, "to understand," in a usage akin to that in the Old Testament book of Daniel, where there is also question of understanding the heavenly secret. *Brq*, elsewhere in Ugaritic, "lightning," here must be the lightning that is connected with Baal's complete temple, as in 4.5.71. *'Abn* is more likely a qal than an aphel, because of its parallel to

"mountain of my *nḥlt*" (3.3.27; 3.4.64) of Baal's mountain, and *ʾarṣ nḥlth*, "land of his *nḥlt*" (5.2.16; 4.8.13-14) of

---

ydʿ and of the similarity of usage in the biblical book of Daniel.

ʾibǵyh. Cassuto relates the word to the Arabic *bǵy* or *nǵy*, "to bubble up," therefore, "I will tell or reveal," Cassuto, *The Goddess Anath*, p. 81, and Ginsberg, *ANET*, p. 136. A more convincing etymology is provided by Hebrew *bʿh*, "to ask" (only in Isa. 21:12, 2x), and esp. Aramaic *bʿh*, "to seek," which also agrees better with the context. Baal does not yet have the temple, so is not in a position to reveal anything. Rather he is about to seek it through Anat's intercession. So he is seeking the temple, the lightning, and all the trappings of royal power. Such an interpretation fits also in 1.3.16 where El is going to arrange with Koshar wa-Khasis for the building of Yamm's palace.

nʿm. The general Ugaritic word for "good" and "pleasant," it is used frequently for external, esp. bodily and sexual beauty. It is used of Lady Hurriya, Anat, and Aqhat. The adjective *nʿmn* in the Krt epic (14. 40, 61, 306; 15.2, 15, 20) and in Nikkal (24.25) has a special use as the favorite or chosen of El. This usage appears to be reflected in the proper names *ʾadnnʿm*, *mlknʿm*, and *nʿmn*. *Nʿm* in this passage refers to a sacred place, parallel with *qdš*. *Nʿm* modifying a place is a common usage in the myths. In 10.3.32, 3.3.28, it refers to Zaphon; in 10.2.30, to the reed marsh of Samka; in 5.6.6, 28; 6.2.19, it refers to the underworld fields of Mot, perhaps euphemistically. *Nʿm* designating a place is

Mot's land and (3.6.16) of Koshar's land. The use of *nḥl* in the economic texts does not help very much. The parallel with *kissi'u ṯibtihu*, "throne on which he sits," and *gib'u tal'iyati*, "hill of victory," shows that *nḥlt* in the myths is a place where power is exercised.

In the Mari archives, which show Amorite usage of the early second millennium, *niḫlatum* is used in the sense of "hereditary property," and the verb *naḫālum* in the G stem, means "to assign (hereditary) property, apportion."[47] In the Hebrew Bible, the meaning of *naḥ^a lāh* is "possession, property, inheritance," while the verb *nāḥal* means "to get or take as a possession." There is a true parallel between the Mari and the biblical usage. *Nḥlt* in both Mari and the Bible is used to mean patrimony as an essentially inalienable piece of land possessed solely by a gentilic unit, large or small.

Nḥlt in Ugaritic describes the territory owned by the god. The *nḥlt* of Mot is where Mot exercises

---

perhaps related to the use of the word in the Krt epic and in proper names. The god has shown favor to a particular place and has set it apart for himself.

47. The verb *naḫālum* is known only from Mari. One passage describes the transfer of landed property from the clan of Awin to Yarim-Addu, probably a senior functionary in the palace of Mari. Yarim-Addu had to go through the fiction of becoming a son of the house of Awin, "these men, sons of Awin, have apportioned (*inḫilu*) the field of Yarim-Addu, their brother," A. Malamat, "Mari and the Bible: Some Patterns of Tribal Organization and Institutions," *JAOS*, 82 (1962), 147-148.

undisputed power over Baal and Baal's messengers. Some understanding of Baal's mountain *ǵr nḥlt* is provided by the parallel *gibʿu talʾiyati*. *Tlʾyt* is from the *lʾy*, "to be strong." The root is found in the epithet of Baal, *ʾalʾiyānu*, a hypocoristicon from the sentence name *ʾalʾiyu qarrādīma*, "I prevail over the heroes" (4.8.34-35; 5.2.10-11, 18), as Albright and F. M. Cross have noted.[48] The *qarrādūma*, "heroes," whom Baal has conquered presumably are the enemies mentioned by Mot (5.1) and by Anat (3.3-4, and *PRU*, II, 3.8-10). According to 3.3.44-4.45 and *PRU*, II, 3.8-10, battles were fought at Zaphon itself. The *gbʿ tlʾiyt* appears to be the hill won by the strength of Aliyan Baal and by Anat--thus the hill of victory. *Ǵr nḥlty*, then, is a mountain possessed inalienably, a patrimony, with the possible overtone of possession by conquest.

Nḥl, usually translated "heir," does not occur in the mythological texts, just as *nḥlt* occurs nowhere else except in the myth texts. In the administrative texts, *nḥl* usually occurs in the formulae of ownership of property, PN *wa-naḥaluhu*, "PN and his *nḥl*." A good example is a list of properties let out for tenant farming: *šd bn ʾlṯtmr bd tbbr w šd nḥlh bd tṯmd*, "The field of the son of *ʾilṯmr* under the management of *tbbr* and the field of his *nḥl* under the management of *tṯmd*" (82.A.11-12). A sequence of "heirs" can be named, as in an account list: *bn tlmyn* $2\frac{1}{2}$ *wnḥlh* $2\frac{1}{2}$ *wnḥlhm 3*, "son of tlmyn $2\frac{1}{2}$ and his

---

48. Albright, *Archaeology and the Religion of Israel*, p. 195, n. 11. Cross, "Yahweh and the God of the Patriarchs," *HTR*, 55 (1966), 254, and n. 126.

nḥl 2½ and their *nḥl* 3" (113.6-8). The *nḥl* appears to be named and to be the tenant farmer in a list of *'ubdy* fields, *šd prn bd 'agpṯn nḥlh*, "the field of Prn under the management of 'agpṯn his *nḥl*" (*PRU*, V, 29.2). Not much light is shed by these texts. The meaning appears to be "heir."

The fuller context of the whole of the tablet adds force to the above argument. We take column 1 to be the victory celebration of Baal after the defeat of his enemies. The well-known ivory from Megiddo, dated by its excavator to 1350-1150 B.C., in which the king feasts and enjoys music while prisoners were brought before him, is a good illustration of column 1 of the third tablet.[49]

Column 2 is a graphic glimpse of Anat fighting in the war which Baal has just won. The messengers tell Anat to call off war and to assume her role as fertility goddess. Baal will then announce to her his victory and the restored harmony of nature to come through his temple.

A parallel to much of this text exists in what is here termed the Baal-Yamm cycle, 1.3. In that instance, El sends his messengers to Koshar wa-Khasis to hasten to him in the same words as *CTA* 3, so that he can give orders to build a temple for Yamm. Almost the same enigmatic language as in the present passage is used--[*rgm 'ṣ wlḫšt 'abn*] *t'unt šmm 'm* [*'arṣ thmt 'mn kbkbm*] *rgm ltd' nš*[*m wltbn hmlt 'arṣ*] *'at w 'ank 'ib*[*ǵyh*--"The speech of wood and the whisper (?) of stone, the converse

---

49. *The Ancient Near East in Pictures*, ed. James Pritchard, 2nd ed. (Princeton, N.J.: Princeton University, 1969), no. 332. Hereafter abbreviated as *ANEP*.

(?) of heaven with the earth, the deeps with the stars, speech which men do not know, and the multitude of the earth do not understand. Come and I will seek it." But here the subject is El. This means that the converse, or meeting, between earth and heaven and the "seeking out," applies to El as well as to Baal. The common element in the contexts of the two passages is the announcement to Anat to lay down arms (in the first passage in 1.2.19-21; in the second, 3.3.11-14), and the command to come to the mountain-dwelling of El or Baal. In the El passage, Koshar wa-Khasis is instructed to build a palace for Yamm. In the Baal passage, Anat goes to El to get permission to build. The element common to both contexts is the building of the temple. It is therefore natural, given the linguistic difficulties of the passage, to look for an explanation in the ideology of the temple.

Apparently the message that El or Baal have to give is simply that they seek to build a temple. The phrase *rgm ʿṣ wlḫšt ʾabn*, "the speech of wood and the whisper (?) of stone," may be related to the cedar and precious stone that went into Baal's temple. The phrase *tʾant šmm ʿm ʾarṣ thmt ʿmn kbkbm*, "the converse (?) of heaven with the earth, of the deeps with the stars," is perhaps to be related to the fact that the palace/temple of the god is at the cosmic center, the meeting place of heaven and earth.

The meaning of the passage in 3.3, therefore, seems to be that Baal has won his victory. He informs Anat, his ally, to put on the face of the goddess of fertility and to hasten to him. A temple which is to celebrate and bring about fertility and cosmic harmony is to be built.

The *'ibǵyh* refers to the seeking out of the temple itself, either by Koshar wa-Khasis or El. Anat will be the agent in the seeking. Baal will seek the temple for his holy place, on the mountain which he has acquired by his victory over the forces of evil.

Type III

ta'li ba-ǵūri m-s-l-mat
ba-ǵūri tal'iyati
wa-ta'lī ba-kī-mā ba'arari
ba-mā 'arari wa-ba-ṣapāni
ba-na'ami ba-ǵūri tal'iyati
(10.3.28-31)

She went up to the mount of . . .
To the mountain of victory
And she went up indeed to 'arr,
To 'arr and to Zaphon,
To the chosen spot, to the hill of victory[50]

---

50. *Philological notes.* The meaning of certain words, the metrics, and, therefore, the parallelism are uncertain in this excerpt. Uncertain letters have a small circle over them. The scribe seems to have been conscious of the metrical problems. An examination of the photograph shows that 1.28 (the first line above) may have been *bkm bǵr* originally and then been corrected--possibly to shorten the line. The *bkm w* in 11.30-31 (third line above) show perhaps an attempt to fill out the meter artificially.

mslmt. It is tempting to relate this word, as Gordon suggests, to the Hebrew hapax *sullām*, "ladder," of Gen. 28:12, of Jacob's ladder which was set upon earth,

The interpretation of *CTA* 10 is extremely difficult. The first column gives no connected sense. In the second, Baal meets Anat in the reed marsh near Lake Huleh and in that place a cow comes on the scene. The third column tells evidently of a *hieros gamos* between Baal and Anat. Anat comes to the mountain to announce to Baal the good news *(bšr)* of offspring for Baal. Although the whole tablet and our text are obscure, the action is clear. Baal receives an announcement on his holy mountain.

Type IV

ba'lu yāṯibu kī ṯibtu ǵūru
Haddu rā['iyu] kī m-d-b
ba-tôki ǵūrihu 'ili ṣapāni
ba-tôki ǵūri tal'iyati
šab'atu baraqīma

---

its top reaching the heavens. However, it does not pair well with *ǵr tl'iyt*.

'arr. Because this word is in apparent parallel to Zaphon, it may well be a place name. The place name *'arr* is mentioned in *PRU*, V, 33.1 and 42.1. *PRU*, V, 76 is a list of men inhabiting various villages. Line 32 runs *b nšm b m'r 'arr*, "among the men in M-'-r 'A-r-r." The Amarna letters mention ^{alu}*a-ra-ru* in the ^{matu}*ga-ri* in a letter of *Mat-Ba'lu* to *Ianḫamu* (*EA* 256.23, 25). So *'arr* in the present passage is probably a place name associated with Baal, like *'ugrt ḫlb* in other texts. Baal was obviously worshiped in manifestations in locales other than Zaphon. The locality of *CTA* 10 is around the Lake of Huleh. One might conjecture that *'arr* is to be found there.

ṯamānētū 'āṣaru ra'atti
'iṣṣu baraqīma
ri'šuhu tappaliyu
ṭallayu bênê 'ênê
'u z-'-r-t tamlulu 'išdêhu
qarnāmi--d/ṣ t 'alêhu
ri'šuhu ba-galaṯi ba-šam[ni

(*Ugaritica*, V; *RS* 24.245, 11.1-7)

Baal is enthroned, yea, (his) seat is the mountain.
Hadad shepherds, yea, (his seat is) the m-d-b
In the midst of his mountain, divine Zaphon,
In the midst of the mountain of victory
Seven lightnings . . .
Eight storehouses of thunder,
The staff lightnings . . .
His head is wonderful.
Dew is between his eyes . . .
. . . his legs.
Two horns . . . above him (on his forehead)
His head is in . . . with oil

T. H. Gaster[51] and L. R. Fisher and F. B. Knutson[52] understand *mdb* as "flood." The obvious parallel is Psalms 29:10, "Yahweh is enthroned on the flood." However the derivation of *mdb* is unclear.

The general vocabulary describing Baal's mountain is familiar from the myths. If it is true that Baal is

---

51. *Thespis*, Harper Torchbook (New York: Harper, 1966), p. 244.

52. "An Enthronement Ritual at Ugarit," *JNES*, 28 (1969), 158, n. 7.

enthroned upon the sea, then the undulating lines beneath Baal's feet in the well-known stele of Ugarit may be Yamm or the waters.

Fisher and Knutson see 11.1-4 as the enthronement after the defeat of Yamm and 11.5-10 as a love song to Baal, comparing Song of Songs 4:10-16. There are some reasons for calling this an enthronement ritual. In the enthronement festival of Babylon, the statue of Marduk was led to a sanctuary called the *akîtu*. A sham battle there reenacted Marduk's victory, which was symbolized by the placing of his statue on "the sea," probably a podium. After the return to Babylon, a sacred marriage was performed. Assuming that this text deals with a statue would account neatly for the mention of the parts of the body of Baal. The anointing with oil, the washing (?), the lyre-playing are all a preparation for love in the Ancient Near East. The mention of all of these actions on the verso of the tablet might indicate that the tablet deals with a sacred marriage of Baal and Anat following Baal's anthronement. There were known to be processions of statues of the gods at Ugarit. *PRU*, II, 106 (*RS* 15.115), 107 (*RS* 15.82) show that statues of gods in the temple and their priests and servants were regularly provided with new vestments.[53]

53. Charles Virolleaud, *PRU*, II (Paris, 1957), xxxi. The procession itself is apparently described in several texts, e.g., *k tʿrb ʿṯtrt šd bt mlk*, "When Athtart enters the field of the house of the king," in *Ugaritica*, V, 9.18 (*RS* 24.263, p. 582), 1.18, and cf. *PRU*, V, 4.10.

Zaphon is a place where messages are delivered to Baal, where Baal works that a temple may be built there. It was stormed by enemies, though they were beaten back by Baal and Anat. No decrees are issued from Baal's mountain. In these features it stands in contrast to El's dwelling, where decrees are issued.

Mot's Dwelling

For the sake of completeness, and because it is sometimes asserted that El's mountain dwelling is in the underworld where Mot also lives, the texts describing Mot's dwelling are included.

There are three descriptions of Mot's dwelling.

’iddaka ’al tattinā panīma
‘imma ǵūri t-r-ǵ-z-z
‘imma ǵūri ṯ-r-m-g
‘imma tillêmi ǵaṣrê ’arṣa
šaʼā ǵūra ‘alê yadêmi
ḫiliba la-ẓāri raḥtêmi
wa-ridā bêta hupṯīti ’arṣi
tissapirā ba-yāridī-mi ’arṣa

(4.8.1-9)

Then set your face
Toward Mount Trǵzz
Toward Mount Ṯrmg
Toward the two hills that stop up the underworld.
Lift up the mountain upon your hands,
The hill upon your palms.
And descend to the pest-house of the underworld.

Be counted among those who go down to the underworld.[54]

CTA 4.7 shows Baal taking possession of his mountain after celebrating his dedicatory feast. He seizes towns evidently as a sign of his kingship, gives permission for the craftsman god Koshar wa-Khasis to install a window, then gives forth his voice in thunder. The land trembles, his enemies flee. Then, after a passage that is broken and unclear, Baal sends his messengers *Gapnu* and *Ugaru* to Mot. The excerpt above is Baal's charge to them.

It is clear from this passage that Mot does not dwell on a mountain but at the base of a mountain. The mountain names, strange and foreign to us, and perhaps made deliberately so for the original hearers, give the impression that Mot's land is far away and well hidden.

ʾiddaka ʾal tattinā panīma
tôki qaritihu H-m-rayya

---

54. *Philological notes: trǵzz, ṯrmg*. Nonsemitic names of obviously remote mountains which are at the entrance of the underworld. In a similar description of Mot's above, *ǵr knkny* occurs (5.5.12-13).

ǵṣr ʾarṣ. Possibilities are Arabic *ǵaḍira*, "thriving," and Arabic *gaḍura*, "to retain, enclose." Albright has suggested the "two mounds at the edge of the underworld," *Archaeology and the Religion of Israel*, p. 198, n. 48. Marvin Pope proposes "mounds that plug the netherworld," *JBL*, 83 (1964), 276.

bt hpṯt. The same expression is used in the Old Testament *bêt ha-ḥopšît* in 2 Kings 15:5 (= 2 Chron. 26:21), to describe where Uzziah spent his leprous days.

m-k kissi'u ṯibtihu

ḫaḫḫu 'arṣu naḥlatihu

(4.8.10-14; 5.2.13-16)

Then set your face

In the midst of his city, Ooze,

Decay, the throne on which he sits,

Slime, the land of his heritage.[55]

The passage is a continuation of text I. Clearly the domain over which Mot rules is a watery place, similar to the Sheol of the Old Testament. The watery nature of Mot's domain contrasts with the desert where Mot also seems to be powerful.

wa-'atta qaḥa 'arapatika

---

55. *Philological notes: Hmry.* Cf. *mah^{a}mōrôt* of Ps. 140:11, "watery depths." The same word is used of Mot's maw, *la yaritta ba-napši bini 'ili-mi Môti /. ba-h-m-rati yadidi 'ili ǵaziri*, "You shall indeed go down the throat of the son of El, Mot / in the watery pit of El's beloved hero."

The psalm of Jonah 2 should be compared with this passage. From Sheol, the psalmist cries out to God. He is in the depths *(m^{e}ṣûlāh)*, the heart of the seas *(l^{e}bab yammīm)*, the river has come over him. The waters and the deep threaten him. Reeds entwine his head at the extremities *(qiṣbê)* of the mountains. The psalm of Jonah seems to show the same land of Mot as the Ugaritic texts, the watery realm of death at the foot of the mountains.

ḫḫ. Cf. Akkadian *ḫaḫḫu*, "spittle, slime."

rūḥīka m-d-līka[56] maṭarīka
ʻimmaka šabʻati ǵalamīka
t̠amānē ḫinzirīka
ʻimmaka pidrayya bitta ʼāri
ʻimmaka ṭallayya bitta rabbi
ʼiddaka panīka ʼal tattin
tôki ǵūri k-n-k-n-y
šaʼa ǵūra ʻalê yadêmi
ḫiliba la-ẓāri raḥtêmi
wa-rida bêta hupt̠īti ʼarṣi
tissapir ba-yāridī-mi ʼarṣi
wa-tidaʻ ʼilu-mi k-m-t-t
yišmaʻ ʼalʼiyānu baʻlu
yiʼhab ʻiglata ba-dabri
parata ba-šadi Šaḥal-mi-môti
šakābu ʻimmannaha šabʻa la-šabʻīma
tašaʻliyu t̠amānē la-t̠amānēyīma
wa-taharanna wa-talidanna Mat̠a

(5.5.6-22)

And as for you, take your clouds,
Your winds, your . . ., your rains.
(Take) with you the seven lads,
The eight boars (= commanders).
(Take) with you Misty One, the Daughter of Bright Cloud,
With you, Dewy One, the Daughter of Showers.
Then set your face
Toward Mount Knkny.

---

56. J. C. de Moor has recently suggested "bolt" for the very puzzling *mdl* in *ZAW*, 78 (1966), 69-71

Lift the mountain upon your hands,
The hill upon your palms.
And descend to the infirmary (?) of the underworld.
Be numbered among those who descend to the under-
world.
And the god (Baal) knew . . . (= he obeyed?)
Aliyan Baal hearkened.
He loved a heifer in the "Outback,"
A cow in the field of Shahal mi-Moti.
He lay with her seventy-seven times,
She helped him mount eighty-eight times,
And she conceived and brought forth the Prince.

The word *šd* can have several different meanings in the Ugaritic texts and deserves further study. (1) "field," in the administrative texts; (2) "steppe" as in Krt, "like locusts on the steppe"; (3) an area of measurement frequently in parallel to *kmn*; (4) a mysterious usage in the phrases, "field(s) of El, of Asherah,"etc.; (5) the underworld steppe.

The last usage, *šd* as "underworld (steppe)," the abode of Mot, is interesting. That *šd* is in the underworld is clear from the following text. Anat says of the dead Baal:

'aṯra Ba'li 'arid ba-'arṣi
'appa 'Anatu tittaliku
wa-taṣūd kulla ǵūri la-kabidi 'arṣi
kulla gib'i la-kabidi šadi-mi
tamǵi ba-na'amayyi 'arṣi dabri
yasamāti šadi šaḥal-mi-môti

(5.6.25-30, cf. 5.6.6-7; 6.2.15-17)

"After Baal I will descend to the underworld,"
Yes, Anat journeyed
And combed every hill to the heart of the underworld,
Every hill to the heart of the (underworld) steppe.
She arrived at the Pleasant Land, the Outback,
The Lovely Field, Shahal-mi-moti.[57]

The dead Baal is clearly in the underworld *(ʾarḍ, ʾarṣ)*, where the steppe is located. *Dbr* is best taken in its root sense of (Australian) "outback." *Nʿmy* and *ysmt* seem to be used euphemistically.

The exact sequence of details in *CTA* 5 is not clear because columns 3 and 4 are too damaged to make much sense. In column 2, Baal descends to the underworld where Mot exercises power. In column 6, Baal is reported to have been found dead in the Pleasant Land, the Outback,

---

57. *šḥlmmt*. Suggestions abound but the difficulties remain. I have vocalized as for "lions of death," which perhaps finds some support in 5.1.14, *pa-napšu napšu labiʾīma*, "and the appetite/maw [of Mot] is the appetite/maw of lions." One ought to compare Sefire A 36 *šḥlyn* (of a curse), "May Hadad sow in them (Arpad and its daughter cities) salt and weeds (?) *(šḥlyn)*." Fitzmyer compares Akkadian *šaḥle* as used in the Annals of Assurbanipal, "The districts of Elam I laid waste, salt and cress (or tares) I strewed thereon." *Šḥlmmt* might then be "cursed field." J. Fitzmyer, *The Aramaic Inscriptions of Sefire* (Rome: Pontifical Biblical Institute, 1967), pp. 15, 53. In the Hittite myth of Illuyanku, the Storm-god sows *saḥlū* over the ruins of the house, *ANET*, p. 126. Yet this would be out of alignment with *nʿmy* and *ysmt*.

the Lovely Field, Shahal-mi-Moti. Column 5 is therefore the summons to Baal and his retinue to descend.

It is noteworthy that instead of the wet and miry underworld of 4.8, the underworld here is the steppe, the "outback." The steppe may be considered as a stage on the way to the underworld.[58]

---

58. Aistleitner sees the underworld thus: entrance (two mountains); (1) City *Hmry*; (2) steppe of Mot; (3) workshop of Koshar wa-Khasis; (4) *'Ablm*, the city of the Moon-god. "Ein Opfertext aus Ugarit (no. 53) mit Exkurs über kosmologischen Beziehungen der Ugaritischen Mythologie," *Acta Orientalia Academiae Scientiarum Hungaricae*, V (1955), pp. 18f. Aistleitner is assuming too much exactitude in mythic geography and too much consistency among the different myths. I would revert to a suggestion made earlier, regarding the distinction between the Baal-Yamm and the Baal-Mot cycle. In the former cycle, one would expect Baal's enemy Sea to dwell in the sea. In *CTA* 1 and 2, which I have termed the Baal-Yamm cycle, the location of Yamm's dwelling is nowhere given. The Baal-Mot cycle seems later than the Baal-Yamm cycle and to be geared more to the agricultural year. The god of death and sterility might best be located in this myth in the arid steppe where there is too little water year-round for cultivation. That is the natural place for his *nḥlt*, the area of his dominion and the seat of his influence. With the mixing that often takes place in oral literature in two epics with the same theme, the watery features of Yamm's abode become attached to Mot's dwelling. Thus Mot's dwelling is both a watery place and an arid steppe.

It is clear that Mot lives not on a mountain but in the underworld at the base of the mysterious mountain(s). There is no indication that El lives in the underworld in the passages we have analyzed.

Anat

Anat, too, lives on a sacred mountain, *'inbb*. Although little can be learned from the descriptions, we include them for completeness.

'appa mit̲ni ragamīma 'argumanna
likā likā 'ananā 'ili-mi
'atumu bušṭumu wa-'ana šanîtī
'u ǵūru lā raḥāqu 'ili-mi
'inb-b la raḥāqu 'ilāniyyīma
t̲inu mit̲padāmi taḥtu 'ênāti 'arṣi
t̲alāt̲u mataḥu ǵayurīma
(3.4.75-80)

Also, I have something I want to say.
Go! Go! Messengers of the god (= Baal).
You are slow and I am swift (?).
Is not (my) mountain distant from El,
'nbb distant from the deities?
Two mithpads under the springs of the earth,
Three wide caves. (?)[59]

---

59. *Philological notes: bštm, šnt.* One can compare tentatively the *polel* of Hebrew *bôš*, "to delay," and Arabic *bassa*; and Syriac *šᵉnā*, "depart," The perfect is stative. The picture is not clear. Perhaps Anat is telling the messengers to leave instantly because they

The meanings of several words are uncertain. The assumption is that the passage was created originally for

---

are slower than she is with her wings and her mountain is a long way from Baal's mountain.

ʾu ǵr // ʾinbb. Not *ʾǵr* with many scholars, since *ʾinbb* is elsewhere called a *ǵr* "mountain," in 13.9. Rather, this is a rhetorical question beginning with *ʾu*, intended to argue that the messengers should leave Anat's mountain immediately to get back to Baal. "Is not [my] mountain far away from El [i.e., from the center of things], and the deities [i.e., the sons of El in the Assembly]?" The *ʾilm* is not Baal but El. This is indicated by the parallel in 1.3.18-21 (as reasonably restored by Herdner), *kptr*] *lrḥq ʾilm ḥkp*[*t lrḥq ʾilnym*]. "Is not Kaphtor distant from El, Memphis distant from the gods?" In the latter passage, El summons Koshar wa-Khasis to himself. The *ʾilnym* are the deities surrounding El, the *puḫru*, whom we see especially in the Baal-Yamm cycle. Grammatically, *-ānu* is the adjectival ending, "the one of," which appears in late Phoenician, *ʾln*. The *yod* is either a second adjectival element or an augmentative. In 6.6.46, *ʾilnym* is in parallel with *rapiʾūma*, the "Hale Ones."

Our two line cliché, *ʾu ǵūru . . . ʾilāniyyīma*, originated probably in the Baal-Yamm cycle, of Koshar wa-Khasis who fits the description better than Anat. It perhaps then came to be applied to any scene of messengers summoning gods.

mṯpd. I have taken it as a *miqtal* formation. Albright translates the phrase as "the two fire-places

Koshar wa-Khasis and then applied to Anat, hence the reference to the underground. A passage from Hittite myth may shed light on the passage. "When Mikišanu [= the messenger of Kumarbi] heard the words, he immediately rose and journeyed under river and earth so that the Sun-god of the gods and the gods of the earth did not see him. And he went down to Sea. Mikišanu began to repeat to Sea the words of Kumarbi. 'Come! The Father of gods, Kumarbi, calls. But the affair in which he calls you is an urgent matter. Come immediately. But come under river and earth so that the Sun-god of the gods and the gods of the earth do not see you.'"[60]

Anat lives on a mountain, *'inbb*, a mountain evidently far from the mountain of El.

> 'idd'aka [la yattinā panīma
> 'imma] 'in . b-b
> ba-'alpi ḥaẓiri [rabbati bêti/kumani
> la-pa]nê anati [yahburā wa-yaqullā
> yišta]ḥwiyannu wa-ya[kabbidannahu]
> (1.2.13-18)

---

under the fountains of the earth," i.e., hot springs. *Mṯpdm* in this translation is derived from **špt/ṯpt*, and related to *mišpᵉtayim* of Gen. 49:14 and Judg. 5:16, Albright, *Yahweh and the Gods of Canaan*, p. 275. It seems rather to be a measure of distance, particularly of distance under the earth.

60. I have translated the German translation of H. G. Güterbock, *Kumarbi* (New York: Europa-Verlag, 1946), p. 32. Transliteration of Hittite on his p. *31. Güterbock has made a considerable number of restorations.

Then they (messengers of El) set face
Toward Inbb.
Through (?) a thousand courts,
Ten thousand houses/acres,
At the feet of Anat they bowed and fell,
They worshiped and honored her.

Note that *'in* and *bb* are separated by a word divider. The messengers of El are sent to tell Anat to call off war and pour peace in the earth. Apparently Yamm has been declared winner by El, and she is to cease and desist from helping Baal.

Inbb is the mountain dwelling of Anat.[61] It is

---

61. Two obscure texts tell us little about Anat's dwelling.

w ʿl ḏrʿ nšrk
wa-rābiṣu la-ǵūrika 'inb-b
k̊t ǵūraka 'anāku yadaʿtî
(13.8-10)

And upon the wing of thy eagle,
And one lying at thy mountain inbb,
Indeed [?] I have known thy mountain.

This is a very obscure part of a hymn to Anat (?).

ʿanatu wa-ʿaṯtartu 'inb-b-ha

Anat and Ashtart to Inbb
(*Ugaritica*, V, 7.20; *RS* 24.244, p. 565)

Ashtart is associated with Inbb only here in Ugaritic texts. The line occurs in a series of gods and their dwellings: (1) *'il mbk nhrm bʿdt thmtm*; (2) *bʿl mrym ṣpn;*

parallel with *ǵr* in 3.4.78. It appears to be far from the mountain of El if the suggestion above is correct. It is a cliché, as can be seen from its use with Koshar. No special characteristics attach to Anat's mountain, as one finds with El's or Baal's dwelling. Perhaps this is an indication that *ʾInbb* plays no special role in the myths. Note the strange expression *ʿnt ṣpn*, "Anat Zaphon," in *Ugaritica*, V, 13.13-14, 17 (*RS* 24.253, p. 592).

Koshar wa-Khasis

The fourth god whose dwelling place is of interest to us is Koshar wa-Khasis, the craftsman god.

> ʾiddaka ʾal tattinā panīma
> tôki Ḥikupti ʾili kullahu
> Kaptori kissiʾi ṯibtihu
> Ḥikupti ʾarṣi naḥlati
> ba-ʾalpi šadi rabbati kumani
> laʾpaʿnê Kôṯari huburā wa-qullā
> tištaḥwiyā wa-kabbidā huwata
> (1.3.1-3)

> Then (messengers of El), set face
> Toward Memphis-of-Ptah,[62] all of it;
> (Toward) Crete, the throne on which he sits,
> Memphis, the land of (his) heritage

---

(3) *dgn ttlh*; (4) *nt wʿṯtrt ʾinbh*; (5) *yrḫ lrgth*; (6) *ršp bbth*, etc. Thus, *ʾinbb* seems to be the standard name for Anat's dwelling.

62. Amarna *Ḫikuptaḫ* for Egyptian *Ḥ(t)-k -Ptḥ*. So Albright, *Yahweh and the Gods of Canaan*, p. 137, and n. 69.

Through a thousand acres, ten thousand hectares.
At the feet of Koshar bow and fall,
Worship and honor him.

In column 2, it may be assumed that Anat has been told to lay down arms because El has declared Yamm the winner over Baal. In this passage, El sends his messengers to summon Koshar to El's mountain. El will then command him to build a temple for Yamm.

No mountain is mentioned. Koshar is to be found in both Crete and Memphis, which is not surprising in view of Ugarit's importation of art objects from these two areas.

wa-ya‘ni Kôṯaru wa-Ḫasīsu
[likā likā ‘anana ’ili-mi]
’atumu buštumu wa-’an[a šanîtī
’u Kaptoru] lā raḥāqu ’ili-mi
Ḥikup[tu lā raḥāqu ’ilāniyyīma
ṯinu miṯpadāmi taḥtu [‘ênāti ’arṣi
ṯalātu matāḥu] ǵayurīma
(1.3.17-21; cf. 3.4.76-80 and 2.3(?)2-3)

And Koshar wa-Khasis answered,
"Go! Go! Messengers of El.
You are slow but I am fast (?).
Is not Kaphtor distant from El,
Memphis distant from the gods?
Two mithpads under the springs of the earth,
Three broad caves. (?)

The context is the same as the preceding passage. Crete and Memphis, the homes of Koshar, are said to be distant from El's mountain, whence come the messengers.

A similar passage describes Anat's mountain dwelling. If the view is correct that the cliché is originally of Koshar, the text is evidence that Koshar has his workshop under the earth.

’alp- . . . yamm-
rabbat- . . . ba-naharêmi
‘-bara gubla ‘-bara q-‘-l
‘-bara ’ihat-nōp-šamūma
šamšir la dāgiyu ’aṯirati
maǵī la qadišu wa’amuru
’iddaka ’al tattina panīma
tôki Ḥikupti ’ili kullihu
Kaptori kissi’i ṯibtihu
Ḥikupti ’arṣi naḥlatihu
ba-’alpi šadi rabbati kumani
la-pa‘nê Kôṯa<r>i hubura

(3.6.5-18)

1000 . . . sea,
10,000 . . . in rivers.
Traverse Byblos, traverse Q‘l.
Traverse Ihat-nop-shamumi.
Proceed, O Fisherman of Asherah,
Advance, O Qadesh and Amur.
Then set your face
Toward Memphis of Ptah, the whole land,
Caphtor, the seat of his rule,
Memphis, the land of his heritage.
From a thousand fields, ten thousand acres,
At the feet of Koshar bow down.

Anat receives permission from El to build Baal a palace. Then she dispatches a servant to the west to fetch Koshar. If El's mountain at Aphaca is the place from where the messenger is sent, then Byblos would actually be the first city on the way to the west.

What is stressed in all the texts regarding Koshar's dwelling is that he lives in the west, in the countries of artisans. He may live in the underworld. More accurately, one may travel to him via an underground route. He does not live on a mountain.

Glyptic Evidence

The evidence of cylinder seals for the cosmic mountain in Canaan must now be considered.

There are a number of cylinder seals,[63] particularly of Hurrian inspiration which may illustrate the cosmic

---

63. Henri Frankfort, *Cylinder Seals* (London: Macmillan, 1939) remains the classic treatment of Ancient Near East seals. References to earlier literature as well as a large number of reproductions may be found there. Since then: Gustavus Eisen, *Ancient Oriental Cylinder and Other Seals*, Oriental Institute Publications, 47 (Chicago: Univ. of Chicago, 1940); Anton Moortgart, *Vorderasiatische Rollsiegel* (Berlin: Mann, 1940); *Corpus of Ancient Near Eastern Seals in North American Collections*, Bollingen Series 14 (Washington, D.C., 1948), 2 vols.; Briggs Buchanan, *Catalogue of Ancient Near Eastern Seals in the Ashmolean Museum* (Oxford: Clarendon, 1962), 2 vols.; M. Vollenweider, *Catalogue raisonné des sceaux cylindres et intailles* (Geneva: no pub., 1967); Ruth Opificius, "Syrische Glyptik der zweiten Hälfte des zweiten Jahrtausends," *Ugarit-Forschungen*, 1 (Neukirchen: Kevelaer, 1969), 95-110.

mountain. The Hittite Storm-god is found upon a divinized mountain in a cylinder seal found at Ras Shamra, which shows the association of the Storm-god with mountains and the clear personification of mountains.[64]

The Hurrian seals are more suggestive. Henri Frankfort sees as one of the most important new features of the Mitannian seals of the Hurrians the introduction of the winged disk and its support.[65] The outstretched wings at the top of a picture, which in Egypt were a solar symbol, are reinterpreted among the Hurrians in Mitanni and elsewhere as a representation of the sky. The earliest datable rendering of the winged disk in a Mitannian monument is the seal of King Shaushattar reproduced immediately below.

---

64. C. F. A. Schaeffer, *Ugaritica*, III (Paris, 1956), p. 24.

65. Frankfort, *Cylinder Seals*, p. 275. Photo courtesy of the Field Museum of Natural History, Chicago.

A development of the cosmic pillar is seen in an Assyrian seal found at Assur, ca. 1000 B.C. (Frankfort), and a Phoenician ivory from the same place dated by De Mertzenfield to the first millennium. In the Assyrian seal, the relation between the god, the "sacred tree," and vegetal life is expressed. The winged disk is the sky. From outstretched hands water pours down into vases. Within this scene, a sacred tree blooms on a mountain, arising out of the same kind of vase that received the heavenly waters.[66]

66. Ibid., p. 213, text-figure 65. Photo courtesy of the Oriental Institute, Univ. of Chicago.

In the Phoenician ivory, a masculine deity whose clothing simulates a mountain holds in his hands a vase with four streams flowing to vases at each corner. The palmettes at each end of the ivory are of Phoenician type. One can see here the conception of the mountain within which is concentrated the mysterious powers of life, the source of life-giving water.[67]

67. E. DeCamps de Mertzenfield, *Inventaire commenté*

The seals and monuments discussed above illustrate the symbolic nature of the mountain in Syria-Palestine in the period under discussion. No particular description of the mountain in the Ugaritic texts appears to be certainly illustrated by any one seal (although the seal and the ivory from Assur are close to El's "two streams"). Rather they may illustrate the mythic and cosmic dimension of the pillar or mountain, that is, it joins the upper and the lower world; in it is contained a superabundance of life, of water; it is the throne of the deity. The seals can thus bring out graphically what the myth texts assume.

An examination of the Ugaritic texts shows that the mountain of both El and Baal can be called cosmic. El's mountain is where the gods meet to decide issues that affect the universe; it seems to be the paradisiac source of water that gives fertility; it is the place where decrees are issued that give ruling power to death-dealing and unruly enemies or to life-giving powers. Baal's mountain is a place of combat in which issues of life and death are decided; it is a place which commemorates victory. As cosmic is defined in Chapter I, these two mountains are cosmic.

---

des ivoires phéniciens et apparentes découverts dans le Proche Orient (Paris: E. de Boccard, 1954), I, 156-157; II, pl. 54. Cf. a similar scene on a late Kassite cylinder of ca. 1350-1200, Buchanan, *Ancient Near Eastern Seals*, p. 102, and pl. 38, p. 562.

III. THE COSMIC MOUNTAIN IN THE OLD TESTAMENT

The land where Israel lived her faith was a land of mountains and highlands as well as of lowlands and desert. From her earliest period as a people, around Sinai, through the time of her settled life, around Zion, sacred mountains played a significant role in Israel's religious life.

This chapter examines the traditions contained in Genesis 2:6-15 and 28:10-22, the Sinai and Zion traditions, then some archaic material in Isaiah and Ezekiel. Finally, cosmic aspects of the Temple furnishings will be studied.

The Genesis Traditions[1]

Genesis 2:6-15

> 6 And a ground-flow (LXX *pēgē*) went up from the earth and it watered the entire face of the earth.

---

1. Gen. 11:1-9, the story of the Tower of Babel, evokes the ziqqurat of Mesopotamia yet has been now thoroughly subordinated to the story of the outworking of human sin that constitutes one of the major themes of Gen. 1-11. The ideology of the ziqqurat is not preserved. Among more recent authors, see F. M. Th. de Liagre Bohl,

7 And Yahweh-Elohim formed the man, dust from the
earth. And he breathed in his nostrils breath of
life. And man became a living being. 8 And Yahweh-
Elohim planted a garden in Eden in the east and he
placed there the man whom he made. 9 And Yahweh-
Elohim caused to bloom from the earth every tree
pleasant to look upon and good to eat. And the tree
of life was in the midst of the garden and the tree
of knowledge of good and evil. 10 And a river went
out *(yōṣēʾ)* from Eden to water the garden and from
there it divided and it became four headstreams.
11 And the name of one was Pishon. It meanders[2]
through the whole land of Havilah, where there is
gold. 12 And the gold of that land is good. There
is bdellium and *shoham*-stone. 13 And the name of the
second river is Gihon. It meanders through the
whole land of Cush. 14 And the name of the third
river is *Hiddeqel* (= Tigris). It flows east of
Asshur. And the fourth river is the Euphrates.

"Babel und Bibel I," *Jaarbericht van het Vooraziatisch-Egyptisch Gezelschap "Ex Oriente Lux"*, 16 (1959/1962), ed. 1964, 103-118, esp. p. 117.

2. For justification, see E. A. Speiser, "The Rivers of Paradise," *Oriental and Biblical Studies*, ed. J. J. Finkelstein and Moshe Greenberg (Philadelphia: University of Pennsylvania, 1967), p. 28. For the latest detailed discussion of Gen. 2:4b-3:24, with extensive bibliography, see Claus Westermann, *Genesis*, BK I[4] (Neukirchen-Vluyn: Verlag des Erziehungsverein, 1970), pp. 245f.

[15]And Yahweh-Elohim took the man and placed him in the garden of Eden to work it and to keep it.

Ezekiel 47:1-12, Zechariah 14:8, and Joel 4:18 (E. VV. 3.18) speak of fertilizing waters flowing *(yṣ')* from the Temple in Jerusalem. The Temple is on Mount Zion. Ezekiel 28 assumes the garden in Eden (v. 13) is the holy mountain (vv. 14, 16). Are the *'ēd*, "ground-flow (v. 6),[3] and the four rivers of Paradise (vv. 10-14) related to the prophetic passages above? Do all the passages reflect the Ugaritic mythological conception that the dwelling of El is the source of the cosmic waters? El lived in a tent next to the *mabbikū naharêmi*, "the source of the two rivers," and the *'apīqū tihām(ā)têmi*, "the pools of the double-deep," as shown in Chapter II.

Scholars generally recognize verses 10-14, describing the four rivers, to be an explanation of verse 6, "a ground-flow came up from the earth and watered the whole land." The four headstreams rose in the Persian Gulf. In the view of the priests and poets of Sumer, the Persian Gulf gave the Tigris and Euphrates their annual overflow, not the mountains of Armenia. There, in the Gulf, was the "mouth of the rivers," that is, where the Tigris and the Euphrates "drank" of the Persian Gulf.[4] Near the head of the Persian Gulf, "the mouth of the rivers,"

---

3. I.e., of the sweet-waters beneath the earth. E. A. Speiser, "*Ēd* in the Story of Creation," *Oriental and Biblical Studies*, pp. 19-22, repr. from *BASOR*, 140 (1955), 9-11.

4. S. N. Kramer, "Dilmun, the Land of the Living," *BASOR*, 96 (1944), 27-28, n. 41.

(sometimes "the mouth of the two rivers") lay Dilmun. This is the "land of the living"--a place without sickness or death, a garden of the gods, paradise. The Genisis account, with its Mesopotamian flavor, reflects this view of a paradise in the east, the source of waters. The number four has been used here to show totality, as for example, the four winds, the four corners of the world. Gihon and Pishon have every appearance of being artificially formed to bring the number of rivers to four.[5]

The river which goes out from Eden in verse 10 appears to be an explanation of the *ʾēd*, "the ground-flow" of verse 6. It may be assumed, then, that the *nāhār* of verse 10 rises from the subterranean sweet water to bring life to the face of the earth. Is this conception related to the "two rivers" of El's dwelling? If El's dwelling can be localized at all from the Ugaritic texts and from Syrian geography, it is Aphaca, modern Khirbet Afqa, in Syria, where the Nahr Ibrahim appears to rise out of a huge cave, as shown in Chapter II. The setting of Genesis 2-3, however, is Mesopotamian, not West Semitic. If there is any borrowing, it is more likely from Mesopotamia in this instance. The location of El's abode at

---

5. *Gîḥôn* is to be formed from *gûaḥ* or *gîaḥ*, "to flow," and *Pîšôn*, from *pûš*, "to jump." So "Gusher" and "Bubbler." So, among many others, Umberto Cassuto, *A Commentary on the Book of Genesis*, pt. I, trans. Israel Abrahams (Jerusalem: The Magnes Press, 1961), p. 116. In this view, the Gihon in Gen. 2 need not be the spring of Jerusalem.

the *mabbikū naharêmi*, "the sources of the two rivers," recalls the *pî nārāti kilallê*, "the mouth of the two rivers," of Akkadian incantation texts, while the *'apīqū tihām(ā)têmi*, "the sources of the double deep," of El finds a parallel in the East Semitic conception of the salt waters of the Persian Gulf being the source of the overflow of the Tigris and the Euphrates.

Less conjectural is the relation between the streams issuing from paradise and the four streams of Mesopotamian art. The motifs of the god with overflowing vase and the god from whose body streams flow are well known.[6] At Megiddo was found a sherd which depicted a palm tree. As the tree of life it takes the place of the deity. A stream flows to the earth in the place of the lower branches on each side.[7] As with all glyptic, literary sources are needed to interpret it. The art can only illustrate the theme. It does not explain the meaning.

Ezekiel 47:1-12, Zechariah 14:8, Joel 4:18 (E. VV. 3.18) all refer to Mount Zion and are rooted in the tradition of a sacred mountain in the north, Zaphon in Syria. Genesis 2:6, 10-14, on the other hand, is rooted in Mesopotamia, "in the east." Though both traditions

---

6. E. Douglas van Buren, *The Flowing Vase and the God with Streams* (Berlin: H. Schoetz & Co., 1933). See Chap. II, sec. on Glyptic Evidence.

7. L. H. Vincent, *Syria*, 5 (1924), 106, pl. xxiv, fig. 1, and van Buren, *The Flowing Vase*, p. 22. Cited in Otto Kaiser, *Die mythische Bedeutung des Meeres in Ägypten, Ugarit, und Israel*, 2nd ed., BZAW, 78 (Berlin: Alfred Töpelmann, 1962), pp. 111-112, n. 100.

speak of life-giving waters issuing from a blessed place, the different regional origins argue against anything except a general similarity. The joining of the theme of the Garden of Eden and of the holy mountain in Ezekiel 28 appears to be late and peculiar to the Ezekielian passage.

Genesis 28:10-22

In explanation of this passage of Jacob's dream at Bethel, the Mesopotamian ziqqurat interpreted as a cosmic center is often invoked.[8]

> [10]And Jacob went out from Beersheba and went toward Haran. [11]And he came to a holy place, and spent the night there because the sun had set. And he took one of the stones of the place and made it his head-rest. And he slept in that place. [12]And he dreamed and
>
> Behold a stairway was set up in the earth,
> And its top reached the heavens.
> And behold, messengers of God
> Went up and down on it.
>
> And he said, "I am Yahweh, the God of Abraham, thy father, and the God of Isaac. The land on which you

---

8. Gerhard von Rad, *Genesis*, trans. John F. Marks (Philadelphia: Westminster, 1961), p. 279, and E. A. Speiser, *Genesis*, Anchor Bible (Garden City, N.Y.: Doubleday, 1964), pp. 218-220. Hermann Gunkel, *Genesis*, 6th ed. (Göttingen: Vandenhoeck & Ruprecht, 1964), though citing many oriental parallels, is unconvinced of Babylonian influence (p. 318).

> are lying I will give to you and to your seed.
> 14 And your seed shall be as the dust of the earth.
> And you shall spread to the west and to the east
> and to the north, and to the south. And by you and
> by your seed shall all the families of the earth
> find blessing. 15 And, behold, I am with you and
> will guard you everywhere you go. And I will bring
> you back to this land. I will not leave you until
> I have done that about which I spoke to you." 16 And
> Jacob awoke from his sleep and said, "Surely, Yahweh
> is actively present in this place and I did not know
> it." 17 And he was afraid and said, "How terrible is
> this place. It is none other than the house of God.
> And this is the Gate of Heaven." 18 So Jacob arose
> early in the morning and took the stone which he had
> set up as a head-rest. And he set it up as a
> *maṣṣēbāh* and poured oil on its top. 19 And he named
> the holy place *Bêt-ʾēl*; the name of the city was Luz
> previously. 20 And Jacob vowed in these words, "If
> God will be with me and will keep me in this way
> which I am walking, and will give me food to eat and
> clothes to wear, 21 and I come again safe to my
> father's house, then Yahweh will be my God. 22 And
> this stone which I have set up as a *maṣṣēbāh* will be
> the house of God. And of all which you give me, I
> will give a tenth to you."

This story, which tells of the origin of the holy place of Bethel, has come down to us in two traditions--the Elohist (vv. 10-12; 17-18; 20-22) and the Yahwist (vv. 13-16; 19a). It is customary to find the influence of the Mesopotamian ziqqurat here. "Gate of Heaven" finds a ready parallel in the folk etymology of "Babylon," *bāb-ilim*, "Gate of the god," and the Babylonian ziqqurat is in a sense a staircase which the god ascends and descends. However, we should not be misled by the Mesopotamian elements in Genesis 1-11 and find similar influence here. The story explicitly tells of the origin and ideology of a Canaanite shrine, the pre-Israelite holy place at Bethel.

Jacob discovers that the deity is present actively, *yēš*, in the place. He acknowledges this effective presence after he experiences it in a dream. One thinks immediately of a Canaanite, rather than a Mesopotamian, analogy. In *CTA* 6.3.1-24, El sees, in a dream, fertility return to the land and proclaims that Baal lives and possesses effective powers.

ba-ḥulumi luṭpāni ʼili dū pāʼidi
ba-ḏ-r-ti bāniyi banuwāti
šamūma šamna tamaṭṭirūna
nahalūma talikū nubta-mi
wa-ʼidaʻu ki ḥayya ʼalʼiyān baʻlu
kī ʼêṯa zubūlu baʻlu ʼarṣi
(6.3.4-9)

In a dream of the Kindly One, El Benign,
In a vision of the Creator of Creatures,
The heavens rain oil,
The wadis flow with honey.
"And I know that Aliyan Baal lives,
That the Prince, Lord of the Earth, exists."

Ugaritic *ʼiṯ* (related to Hebrew *yēš*) means "to be," but in cultic contexts has a much stronger force, "to be present with power." This passage should also be compared with the enigmatic passage in Ugaritic,

> rigmu ʿiṣṣi wa-l-ḫ̆-š̌-t ʾabni
> t-ʿan-t šamīma ʿimma ʾarṣi
> tihāmātu ʿimma-ni kabkabīma
>
> (3.3.19-22)
>
> The speech of wood and the whisper of stone,
> The converse (meeting?) of heaven with earth,
> Of the deeps with the stars.

Apparently, the cosmic function of Baal's temple is the subject. Baal's temple and kingship will bring fertility and cosmic harmony. If this is the function of the heavenly temple, it is also the function of the earthly shrine which re-presents the heavenly sphere. The Canaanite parallels serve to clarify the meaning of the stairway between heaven and earth. Like Baal's mountain temple, it brings about cosmic harmony and facilitates relations between man and the high god of the shrine. Although it is likely that the story in Genesis 28 originally concerned the Canaanite high god El and not Baal, the ideology operative in the shrines of either god would be similar.

The meaning of the *maṣṣēbāh* is not clear.[9] Jacob expressly says it will be the house of God. The *stēlē*, as the Septuagint translates *maṣṣēbāh*, was a feature of Canaanite religion as we know from many Old Testament

---

9. For the most recent treatment, see Carl F. Graesser, "Studies in Maṣṣēbôt" (unpub. diss., Harvard University, 1970).

passages and Philo Byblios. In Eusebius' *Praeparatio Evangelica,* 1.10.10, *Ousōon* consecrates two pillars to fire and to wind. He worships them and pours libations of blood upon them from the wild beasts he had killed in the hunt.

There are other parallels in Ugaritic. Krt makes a vow at the shrine of Asherah of Tyre and Elath of Sidon to make a payment of gold and silver (14.4.197-206), just as Jacob vows a tithe. In the same epic, El promises success and progeny to Krt in a dream. Krt's response is to sacrifice to El and to Baal (14.1-2). In a Canaanite setting the *malʾakê ʾelōhîm* would be either the messengers of the gods (probably a pair in Ugaritic) or the sons of El, the assembly of El. In Krt, the assembly plays a role in blessing the favored human being (15.2.4-28; 3.2-19). The assembly of the gods *(ʿdt, pḫr, mpḫrt, bn ʾil)* plays a role in the Ugaritic mythology and always had an important place in the Phoenician pantheon in the first millennium.

The Bethel story, therefore, tells of the origin of an important El shrine in Canaan and, in so doing, tells how a Canaanite shrine operates. It has been inserted into the patriarchal story of the promise, and the attitude of Jacob towards these acts of God is highlighted.

Sinai Traditions

In the early traditions of Israel regarding the Exodus from Egypt, the giving of the Law, and the wandering prior to the Conquest, Yahweh-Elohim is associated closely with a mountain. It is called Sinai in the Yahwist (J) and Priestly (P) strands and Horeb in the

Elohist (E) and Deuteronomic (D) traditions. In all four traditions, J, E, D, P, the mountain where Yahweh gave the Law to Israel through Moses is sometimes called "the mountain (hā-hār)." Only in E and P is it called "the Mountain of God *(har hā-ʾelōhîm)*."[10]

Different traditions have attached themselves to the different names of the mountain of law-giving. The traditions surrounding each name will be examined.

Sinai

Even the general location of Sinai cannot be established with certainty from the evidence now available.[11] The early poems telling of Yahweh's "March in the South." Deuteronomy 33:2-3; Habakkuk 3:3-7; Judges 5:4-5, indicate that Sinai is to be found in Seir and Edom in the rugged mountain area southeast of the Dead Sea. Despite

---

10. In a unique passage in the Pentateuch, Num. 10:33, Sinai is called "the Mountain of Yahweh." The word *ṣûr*, "rock, crag," never means the mountain of law-giving.

11. See G. E. Wright, "Sinai, Mount," in *Interpreter's Dictionary of the Bible*, IV (New York: Abingdon, 1962), 376-378, for brief discussion of the location of Sinai. (Hereafter abbreviated as *IDB*.) A thorough examination of the traditions of the location of Sinai can be found in Jean Koenig, "La Localisation du Sinai et les traditions des scribes," *RHPR*, 43 (1963), 2-31, and 44 (1964), 200-235. Koenig unfortunately lays too great stress on the assumed volcanic activity of Exod. 19, and pays insufficient attention to the form of theophany in a storm.

uncertainty about the location of Mount Sinai, the literary traditions about Sinai can be classified into three types according to language and context.

The first type, *midbar Sînay*, "the wilderness of Sinai," occurs eleven times. This exclusively Priestly use, which does not associate a mountain with Sinai, is always in the chronological or structural framework of a journey. "Wilderness of Sin *(midbar Sîn)*" occurs four times in a similar journey framework, again in P. *Sînay* may be a development from *Sîn* by the addition of the *-ayu* suffix, signifying "the one of." In this view, *Sînay* would be "the one (that is, mountain) of the Wilderness of Sin." *Sînay* could then develop into the name of the mountain and then back to the name of the wilderness alongside the older, more original, *Sîn*.

"Mount Sinai *(har Sînay)*," the place of law-giving, is used seventeen times. The phrase is nearly always "Mount Sinai" and Moses is always central--in contrast to the Horeb traditions where "mountain *(har)*" is used only three times in seventeen uses of Horeb and where the people generally play a large role, not Moses.[12]

Several important passages in the Book of Exodus deal with Mount Sinai.

> And Yahweh said to Moses, "Behold I am coming to you in a chariot of cloud *(ʿab heʿānān)*.[13] (Exod. 19:9a E)

---

12. Usually the phrase is "at Horeb *(bᵉḤōrēb)*." And Horeb seems more precisely located than Sinai (Deut. 1:2; 1 Kings 19:8).

13. Yahweh makes the *ʿābîm* his chariot and goes on

> And Moses came down from the mountain to the people and he sanctified the people and they washed their garments. And he said to the people, "Be ready by the third day. Do not go near a woman." And on the third day in the morning, there was thunder and lightning and a dark cloud *(ʿānān kābēd)* upon the mountain and a very loud trumpet blast, and all the people who were in the camp trembled. And Moses brought the people out of the camp to meet God and they assembled at the foot of the mountain. And Mount Sinai was all smoke because the Lord descended upon it in fire; and the smoke of it went up like the smoke of a kiln. And all the people trembled greatly. And as the trumpet blast grew louder and louder, Moses spoke and the Lord answered him in thunder. And Yahweh came down upon Mount Sinai to the top of the mountain. And Yahweh called Moses to the top of the mountain and Moses went up. (Exod. 19:14-20 J-E)

> And all the people perceived the (thunder)peals and the (lightning)flashes and the trumpet blast and the mountain smoking. The people were afraid and trembled and stood at a distance. (Exod. 20:18 E)

> And Moses and Aaron, Nadad, and Abihu and seventy of the elders of Israel went up and they saw the God of Israel. And beneath his feet, there was, as it were, a pavement of lapis-lazuli like heaven itself for

---

the wings of the wind in Ps. 104:3. Isa. 19:1 shows Yahweh mounting a swift cloud, *rōkēb ʿal ʿab qal*.

> brightness. And he did not lay his hand on the chief men of the people. They beheld God and ate and drank. (Exod. 24:9-11 J)

> And the cloud covered the mountain. And the Glory of Yahweh tented upon Mount Sinai. And the cloud covered it six days. And he called to Moses on the seventh day from the midst of the cloud. And the sight of the Glory of the Lord was like a devouring fire at the top of the mountain in the eyes of the children of Israel. And Moses entered the cloud and went up to the mountain. And Moses was on the mountain forty days and forty nights. (Exod. 24:15b-18a P)

The descriptions of the coming of the Lord upon the mountain in 19:14-20 and 20:18 have been taken by many commentators to describe the coming of God in an earthquake and volcano. This is highly unlikely. Volcanoes in historical times are attested neither for the Sinai peninsula nor for the Seir-Edom area, more plausible locations for Mount Sinai than present-day Saudi Arabia. Furthermore, the fire of volcanoes goes upward and does not descend from the sky. The passage is rather a description of a theophany in a storm, an amply attested Canaanite tradition. The deity discloses himself in thunder and lightning, both in Ugaritic myth (4.5.69-71; 4.7.25-48) and in the Hebrew Bible. Clouds accompany Yahweh when he appears and accompany Baal, often called the "rider of the clouds *(rkb ʿrpt)*" (4.5.70 and 5.5.6-7). The sound of the horn in the Sinai pericope is perhaps a liturgical imitation of the sound of the wind blowing among the mountains[14] or of thunder.

Yahweh was accompanied by the *ʿānān*, "cloud," on Mount Sinai. In Ugaritic, *ʿnn* is a messenger of the deity, a cloud in all likelihood. Baal had natural elements such as cloud, wind, rain in his entourage who were summoned with him to the underworld (5.5.7-8). In the passage from Exodus, the *ʿnn* has apparently been demythologized, a procedure paralleled in other Old Testament theophanies (Habakkuk 3:5; Psalm 97:2-3). Moses and the elders go up (*ʿlh* as Anat to Zaphon in 6.1.5 and 10.3.18-19), they worship *(hištaḥᵃ wîtem)*, the verb used in Ugaritic of those who approached the dwelling of a god. Beneath the feet of God was a construction of bricks of what was probably lapis lazuli, like the very heavens for clearness. In Baal's palace in Zaphon, there were bricks (*lbnt* 4.4.62,73). There was also lapis lazuli; *ʾiqnʾu* is the Ugaritic equivalent of Hebrew *sappîr*.

wa-bini bahatī kaspi wa-ḫarūṣi
bahatī ṭahāri-mi ʾiqnuʾīma
(4.5.80-81)

And build a house of silver and gold
A house of the clearness of lapis lazuli.

Moses and the elders "ate and drank," apparently a feast on the mountain like those given by Baal and El (for example, 3.1.1-17; 4.4.31-38; 4.6.41-59). Finally, authoritative decrees are issued on Mount Sinai. This

---

14. Umberto Cassuto, *A Commentary on the Book of Exodus*, trans. Israel Abrahams (Jerusalem: The Magnes Press, 1967), p. 232.

recalls the *taḥumu* of El, which was suggested in Chapter II to have been begun to be hypostatized in Ugaritic mythology. The Exodus passages that have been analyzed, then, in their original poetic form, belong to the Canaanite religious tradition of theophany in a storm, on a mountain.

Can one be specific as to the origin in Canaanite religious tradition of the Sinai motifs under discussion? In the Ugaritic texts, Baal-Hadad is the Storm-god who thunders in the mountain while El is the god who dwells in the divine assembly on the mountain, and lives in a tent. El issues decrees. It is impossible to decide whether in the Sinai traditions in Exodus a mixing of language connected with El and Baal has taken place, or whether it is wholly El language.

The theophany language of Exodus is used again in ancient poetry such as Psalm 18:8-20 (= 2 Samuel 22:8-20); Psalm 29; Habakkuk 3:3-15; Psalm 68:8-9; Judges 5:4-5. The language of storm theophany, evocative of Sinai, figures prominently in hymns such as Psalm 50.

> The God of Gods, Yahweh,
> Spoke and summoned the earth
> From the rising of the sun to its setting.
> From Zion, the perfection of beauty,
> Yahweh shone forth *(hôpîʿ)*.
> Our God comes and he will not be silent.
> Before him is a devouring fire,
> Around him is a raging tempest.

Psalm 50.1-3 seems a deliberate attempt to evoke the Sinai encounter in the cult of Jerusalem. The epiphany of Yahweh on Sinai, actualized in the Jerusalem Temple, continues on in Israelite tradition.[15] It seems clear, therefore, that Yahwist and Elohist traditions in Exodus regarding Mount Sinai borrow motifs associated with the idea of the sacred mountain in Canaan.

Sinai occurs in a third type, a group of passages in the Hebrew Bible, all of them in archaic poetry, in which Yahweh with his train comes from his mountain home to aid his people. These can be called the "March in the South" passages after the locale--the mountain country to the south (and east) of Israel. In these passages, Canaanite themes of the sacred mountain can be discerned more easily than in the other Sinai passages. *Sînay* occurs four times in the passages (Deut. 33:2; Ps. 68:9; E. VV. v.8; Ps. 68:18; E. VV. v.17; Judg. 5:5). All the "March in the South" passages will be discussed here.

> 2 Yahweh came from Sinai.
> He beamed forth from Seir upon us.
> He shone forth from the mountain country of Paran.
>
> With him were myriads of Holy Ones.
> At his right hand proceeded the gods (?)
> 3 Yea, the purified of the people.
>
> All the Holy Ones are at thy right.
> They prostrate themselves at thy feet.

---

15. Sigmund Mowinckel, *The Psalms in Israel's Worship*, trans. D. R. Ap-Thomas (New York: Abingdon, 1967), I, chap. V, esp. pp. 156-158; Artur Weiser, *The Psalms*, trans. H. Hartwell (Philadelphia: Westminster, 1962), pp. 393-395; Herbert Schmid, "Yahwe und die Kulttraditionen von Jerusalem," *ZAW*, NS, 26 (1955), 168-197.

They carry out thy decisions.[16]

(Deut. 33:2-3)

The scene described is a theophany of Yahweh from the mountainous regions of the south or southeast. He is present in the midst of his entourage, the holy beings whom Israel demythologized. In what we have termed the

---

16. I have followed in the main the interpretation of F. M. Cross, "Studies in Ancient Yahwistic Poetry" (unpub. diss., Johns Hopkins University, 1950). For *ḥbb* as "purified," Akkadian *ebēbu*, "clean," see Cross, "The Divine Warrior in Israel's Early Cult," *Biblical Motifs*, ed. A. Altmann (Cambridge, Mass.: Harvard, 1966), p. 26. I translate *har Pā'rān* as "the mountain country of Paran," instead of the usual "Mount Paran" for the following reasons: (a) Sinai, with which *har Pā'rān* is in parallel, is nowhere called "Mount Sinai" in the "March in the South" passages. (b) This passage and Hab. 3:3 are the only instance of *har* with Paran of the 12 instances of Paran in the Old Testament. In the epic and historical sources, it is *midbar Pā'rān*. As is well known, *har* can mean a specific mountain or a mountainous terrain. Given the vagueness of the location of the mountain from which God appears, and the fact that *har* occurs only in parallel with Sinai in the "March in the South" passages, we may conclude that the writer had no specific mountain in mind, but a mountainous territory. The fact that Seir and Paran in Deut. 33:2, Seir and the region *(śādeh)* of Edom in Judg. 5:4, and Teman and the mountain country of Paran in Hab. 3:3, are all used to describe whence Yahweh comes, shows these archaic poems envisioned no specific mountain as Yahweh's seat.

Baal-Yamm cycle (*CTA* 1 and 2), and in the Krt texts, El is found in the midst of the divine assembly, *puḫru mô‘idi*, the *‘adatu ʾili-mi*. The sons of El or assembly of El are mentioned in the liturgical texts. They are never seen, however, on the march in holy war in Ugarit, as is the case in the "March in the South" passages.

Psalm 68 has further references to the "March in the South" theme. The psalm itself is notoriously difficult in its structure and its text.[17]

> Yahweh
> When thou didst go out before thy people,
> When thou didst stride through the desert,
> The earth quaked, the heavens dripped (?)
> Before Yahweh, the One of Sinai,
> Before Yahweh, the God of Israel.
>
> (Ps. 68:8)

This passage is to be compared with Judges 5:4-5, which it closely resembles. Both passages probably refer to the early holy wars Israel fought to take or retain possession of the land. Yahweh marches at the head of Israel's armies. Earth and heaven quake at his coming. The scene is set in the desert, rather than at a specific mountain.[18]

---

17. W. F. Albright, "A Catalogue of Early Hebrew Lyric Poems," *HUCA*, 23 (1950), 1-34, has made the plausible suggestion that Ps. 68 is a collection of about 30 *incipits*, from the 13th to the 10th century.

18. I have replaced *ʾelōhîm* in the phrase *ʾelōhîm zeh Sînay* with the more original *Yhwh zeh Sînay*, "Yahweh the One of Sinai."

The chariots of Yahweh were two myriad,
Thousands the archers of my Lord.
They come from Sinai with the Holy Ones[19]
(Ps. 68:18)

Here again, Yahweh the Warrior God, comes from his dwelling place in Sinai, presumably to fight for Israel.

4 Yahweh, when thou didst come from Seir,
When you didst stride from the steppe of Edom.
The earth quaked, the heavens dripped,
Yea, the clouds dripped water.
5 The mountains dripped before the One of Sinai.[20]
(Judg. 5:4-5)

In the two instances of Seir in the "March in the South" passages, it is in parallel with "the mountain country of Paran," Sinai, and the steppe of Edom. This usage differs from the usage in the prophets, the Jahwist and Elohist sources, and the historical books where it is the dwelling place of the sons of Esau and the Horites.

God comes from Teman,
And the Holy One from the mountain country of Paran.
His glory covers the heavens,
And his praise fills the earth.

---

19. *Šin'ān* is to be connected to Ugaritic *ṯnn*, a class of warriors, probably archers in chariots, W. F. Albright, "Early Hebrew Lyric Poems," p. 25. *Qdš* is taken as collective.

20. For a recent study, and bibliography, see Edouard Lipiński, "Juges 5.4-5 et Psaume 68.8-11," *Biblica*, 48 (1967), 185-206.

. . . . .

. . . . .

. . . . .

Before him goes pestilence,
And plague goes forth at his feet.
He stood and shook (?) the earth.
He gazed and made nations tremble.
Everlasting mountains broke up,
Eternal hills collapsed,
Eternal orbits were shattered.
I saw the tents of Cushan,

. . . . .

The curtains of the land of Midian.[21]

(Hab. 3:3-6)

---

21. W. F. Albright divides these verses from vv. 8-15, which tell of Yahweh's combat with River/Sea. Verses 3-7 were probably taken with little alteration from a very early Israelite poem on the theophany of Yahweh in the southeast storm. The historico-geographical background reflects the period following the wilderness wanderings. Verses 8-15 with their Canaanite background reflect the theophany of Yahweh in the northern thunderstorm with its torrent of water. So Albright in "The Psalm of Habakkuk," in *Studies in Old Testament Prophecy*, ed. H. H. Rowley (Edinburgh: T. & T. Clark, 1950), pp. 1-18. It seems more reasonable to assume a unity here. In other "March in the South" passages, the coming of Yahweh was a coming in holy war with the forces of nature involved, as in vv. 8-15.

The above "March in the South" passages all appear to be archaic in meter, vocabulary, and ideas.[22] The most natural historical setting for these hymns is the very early period when Israel was militarily engaged in these areas, in the pre- or early conquest period. Yet we should note a curious thing in these hymns--Yahweh never marches through Palestine. The march is not from the south to the center of Palestine. Rather, the march begins and ends in the south--a march *in* the south rather than from the south. It ought to be concluded, then, that the god of these hymns is a god worshipped in the area of Seir, Edom, Paran, Teman, and Sinai. We know that there were pre- or proto-Israelite leagues in the area. It is natural to assume that the god who marches in these hymns is the god of these leagues.

Yahweh is not associated with individual mountains in these passages. It is true that in Deuteronomy 33:2 and Habakkuk 3:3, *har Pāʾrān* is the place from which Yahweh comes. In the light of other uses of Paran and the parallels with Teman, *śᵉdēh ʾᵉdôm* and Seir, this may be taken as the hill country of Paran. Sinai is not here called a mountain and could just as easily be understood as the wilderness of Sinai. Surprising as it may seem, the "March in the South" should be "the march in the southern mountain area."[23]

---

22. For techniques of dating the early poetry, see most recently, W. F. Albright, *Yahweh and the Gods of Canaan* (Garden City, N.Y.: Doubleday, 1968), chap. i.

23. In Isa. 63:1, "Who is this that comes from Edom?" the "March in the South" theme reappears in sixth

Sinai traditions have been seen to fit into the Canaanite storm theophany. One thinks immediately of Baal in the Ugaritic texts who celebrates his kingship with thunder and lightning from his mountain and who wars against monsters. Certain features, however, indicate that the Canaanite god, El, rather than Baal, may stand behind these passages. Authoritative decrees, the "ten words," and the judgments are issued by God on Mount Sinai, recalling the power-filled *tḥm* of El. Recent studies have pointed out the influence of El upon Yahweh.[24] In Philo Byblius El is a bold and bloody warrior (*Praeparatio Evangelica,* I. 10.16-29). The worship of El seems to have been particularly strong in South Canaan where the "March in the South" passages are at home.[25] As will be seen, the Tent of Meeting finds its best explanation as the earthly copy of El's mountain tent. Although argument will be made for a mixing of El and Baal language in Israel's later history (partly as a result of the transfer of Sinai motifs to Zion-Zaphon), it is better to locate Sinai and its motifs in the tradition of the Canaanite high god, El.[26]

---

century dress. God "strides" (reading *ṣʿd* with the Syriac and Vulgate) as he does in the archaic versions of the same theme. In the Isaian passage, the stress is on the Divine Warrior and his blood-spattered clothes.

24. F. M. Cross, "Yahweh and the God of the Patriarchs," *HTR*, 55 (1962), 225-259.

25. Patrick D. Miller, "El the Warrior," *HTR*, 60 (1967), 411-431, esp. 428-431.

26. Sinai is mentioned infrequently outside of the

Horeb

The equivalent of Sinai in the Elohist and Deuteronomic sources, Horeb has a diversity of settings. Only once does "*Mount* Horeb *(har ḥōrēb)*" occur (Exod. 33:6). In Exodus 3:1, Moses comes to the mountain of God, to Horeb *(ḥōrēbāh)*, and in 1 Kings 19:8, Elijah went forty days and forty nights to the mountain of God, Horeb. In the other fourteen uses, no word for mountain is used with Horeb. Exodus 17:6 is only an apparent exception, since it merely locates the rock whence flowed the water at Horeb. Ordinarily Horeb is a location in the desert in the phrase "at Horeb" *(beḤōrēb)*.

Horeb is associated with the following traditions. It is the place of revelation where God spoke to the people from the midst of fire (Deut. 4:15), the scene of the covenant (Deut. 4:10; 5:2; 28:69; 1 Kings 8:9; Ps. 106:19). In these passages, God deals directly with the people, and not through Moses. Only in Deuteronomy 18:16, Malachi 3:22 (E. VV. 4.4) is Moses the mediator. Horeb secondly is the scene of conflict stories (Exod. 17:6; 33:6; Ps. 106:19; Deut. 9:8). In fact, in Exodus 17:6, the rock *(ṣûr)* which was the scene of the faultfinding of the children of Israel, is specifically located at Horeb. Horeb finally is used three times in descriptions of the

---

Sinai pericope and the "March in the South" passages. The reason is that Yahweh picked Zion and not another sacred mountain. The Sinai epiphany is to occur in Jerusalem, e.g., Ps. 50 and Ps. 97. So Herbert Schmid. "Jahwe und die Kulttraditionen von Jerusalem," *ZAW*, NS, 26 (1955), 189-190.

stages in the wanderings of the wilderness (Deut. 1:2, 6, and 19).

Horeb, therefore, is not simply the Elohist and Deuteronomic counterparts of Sinai in the Yahwist and Priestly traditions. It does not appear to be a mountain at all. It is rather an indefinite location which has gathered certain traditions of the wandering to itself.

Besides Sinai and Horeb, "the mountain *(hā̆-hār)*" and "the mountain of God *(har ʾᵉlōhîm)*" are used to designate the holy mountain of law-giving in the Pentateuch. *Har* with the definite article appears in all four Pentateuchal strands, Jahwist, Elohist, Deuteronomic, and Priestly. It does not seem to be used independently of the Sinai and Horeb traditions as another designation of the mountain of law-giving. In the Elohist tradition "the mountain of God" is found four times. One time, in 1 Kings 19:8, it is used of Elijah's journey to "Horeb, the mountain of God." It has already been noted that Horeb is only once designated as a mountain in the construct relationship *har ḥōrēb* (Exod. 33:6), in contrast to the frequent *har Sînay*. The use in the Elohist tradition of both *har ʾᵉlōhîm* and *ḥōrēb* seemingly as a name for a place rather than for a mountain may indicate the uncertainty of E vis-à-vis the mountain.

Some of the traditions that have attached to Mount Sinai appear to have come from the traditions surrounding the mountain dwellings of Canaanite deities, probably El or Baal. The volcano theory of Sinai should be abandoned in view of unattested volcanic activity in the areas concerned and because of the Canaanite storm-theophany parallels we now have. The use of Canaanite themes for Sinai indicate that Israel was working out its Yahwistic faith in contact with Canaanite religion long before the Conquest.

The Tent in the Desert[27] *and the Tent of El*

In the Priestly account of the building of the Tabernacle *(miškān)* and its equipment, Moses is told to make it according to the pattern *(mišpāṭ* or *tabnît)* shown him on the mountain (Exod. 26:30; cf. 25.9, 40; 27.8 and Num. 8:4). The text is ambiguous as to whether Moses was presented with a plan of the tent or whether he actually saw and copied the heavenly tent. At any rate, it is clear that the tent that Moses had built is a copy of the heavenly tent in accordance with the ancient religious principle, "like is like." The similarity in form between the earthly dwelling of the god and its heavenly prototype brings about the presence of the deity.[28] In Israel, of

---

27. For a good introduction to the problems of the Tent, one should consult, besides the encyclopedias, R. de Vaux, "Arche d'Alliance et Tente de Réunion," in *Bible et Orient* (Paris: Cerf, 1967), pp. 261-276. Some Ugaritic parallels are suggested in Cassuto, *Book of Exodus*, pp. 321-324, and R. J. Clifford, "The Tent of El and the Israelite Tent of Meeting," *CBQ*, 33 (1971), 221-227.

28. Cassuto, *Book of Exodus*, p. 322. That the principle of "like is like" was operative in regard to heavenly and earthly dwellings is indicated by Schaeffer's findings relative to the Baal temple excavated at Ras Shamra. The temple of Baal had a window in the roof, as did Baal's temple on Mount Zaphon. C. F. A. Schaeffer,

course, the presence of Yahweh was subject to a number of conditions, yet the principle of "like is like" seems imperative here, too.

It has been customary to explain the tent in Israel's early traditions by comparing Arabic institutions, especially the *qubbah*, the preislamic camel-borne tent used in processions, oracles, and war-making.[29] Yet in view of what we have seen of the tent of El, it is worth asking if the early Israelite tent is related to the tent dwelling of the god El in the Ugaritic myths.

There are a number of indications that the *miškān* and the *ʾōhel môʿēd* of Israel are the counterparts of the divine dwellings that are found in the Ugaritic texts.

In the Krt epic, the gods live in tents.

ta'tiyū 'ilūma la-'ahalīhumū
dāru 'ili la-miškanātihumū
(15.3.18-19)

The gods go to their tents,
The circle of El to their tabernacles.

In the stereotyped descriptions of El's dwelling at the source of the Double-Deep, El lives in a tent-shrine of some kind.

The Cuneiform Texts of Ras Shamra-Ugarit (London: Oxford, 1939), pp. 66f.

29. F. M. Cross, "The Priestly Tabernacle," *BA*, 10 (1947), 45-68, repr. in *BAR*, I (Garden City, N.Y.: Doubleday, 1961), 210-228, and R. de Vaux, *Ancient Israel*, trans. J. McHugh (New York: McGraw-Hill, 1961), pp. 294-301, 540. A good bibliography on the *qubbah* can be found in de Vaux, "Arche d'Alliance et Tente de Réunion," p. 57, n.2.

tagliyu ḏadī 'ili wa-tabā'u
qarašī malki 'abī šanīma
(3.5.15-16; 4.4.23-24; 6.1.34-36;
2.3.5; 17.6.48-59; 1.3.23-24)
He opened the tent(s) of El and entered
The tent-shrine of the King, the Father of Year.

A Hittite version of a Canaanite myth represents El as living in a tent, as seen in Chapter II. Israel's early traditions represent Yahweh manifesting himself in a *miškān* and *'ōhel*.

Upon the Tent in Israel would rest the cloud *(haʿānān)*. The Yahwist and Elohist traditions are particularly fond of *ʿānān* for the theophanic cloud. In Ugaritic, *ʿnn* is the messenger(s) of the gods, evidently the divinized cloud in their entourage. In Israel, the attendant of the god has seemingly been demythologized into a mere cloud. Israel's tent has a court *(ḥāṣēr)* (Exod. 27.9, 16). The *ḥṣr* is part of Baal's house (4.4.51; 4.5.63; 3.5.47 and elsewhere).[30]

Qrš is used in Ugaritic texts to describe El's dwelling where it means, probably in the plural, "tent(s)"

---

30. In 3:5.46-50; 4:1.13-19; 4:4.50-57, *bt* // *ḥẓr*, "temple // court," are possessed by other gods but not by Baal. Baal seeks a *bt* and *ḥẓr* for himself. Contrasted with temple and court are the *mṯb* // *mẓll*, "dwelling // shelter," where El lives and where Baal and his consorts have to live. Two types of dwellings may well be contrasted in the Ugaritic texts, *bt* and *ḥẓr* being more permanent structures while *mṯb* and *mẓll* are more temporary and mobile, perhaps tents or portable pavilions.

and in the Old Testament, to describe a part of the Tabernacle. The Old Testament use is not altogether clear, but apparently it describes the wood frame on which the tent fabrics were hung. The basic meaning of the Ugaritic word seems to be "frame (of tent)," and hence could be easily used for "tent," by metonymy.

The Tent of Israel is to be made by the divinely commissioned and gifted craftsman Bezalel (Exod. 31:3). The Temple of Baal is made by the craftsman-god Koshar wa-Khasis, "skillful and understanding," *hayyānu dū ḥarašu yadêmi*, "The Skillful One, who is a trained worker" (3.6. 21-23).[31] In Exodus 28:33-34, the skirts of the priest are to have golden bells and pomegranates suspended from the edge. The dress of the priest is considered to be part of the equipment of the Tent. At Ras Shamra, a circular pedestal of bronze has been found, under the rim of which were decorations shaped like pomegranates. These were suspended like the pomegranates on the priestly garment in Exodus 28. A mold for the making of metal ornaments decorated with a row of pomegranates hanging from them along their entire length has been found at Ras Shamra.[32]

---

31. *Hyn* is best related to Hebrew *hôn*, "ability, wealth," Jewish-Aramaic *hawnā*, "skill, ability." *Hawnā* is used in the Targum to Prov. 28:16 to translate *t^ebûnāh*, and *t^ebûnāh* is the quality of Bezalel, the builder of the Israelite tent (Exod. 31:3). Pope, *Wörterbuch der Mythologie*, ed. H. W. Haussig (Stuttgart: Ernst Klett, 1965), 1, p. 296.

32. Schaeffer, *Cuneiform Texts of Ras Shamra-Ugarit*, pl. 23, 2, and pl. 19, 2. Also in *ANEP*, no. 588.

El issued his decree *(ṯḥm)* from his tent.

Old texts in the Hebrew Bible speak of the Tent of Meeting as an oracular tent (Exod. 33:7-11; Num. 11:16-30; 12:4-10). We can see then the similar background and *Ideenwelt* of the tent of El and the Tent of Meeting in Israel's early period.[33]

ʼap maṯni ragamīma
ʼargumaka šaškan maʻ

maggini rabbati ʼaṯirati yammi
maǵaẓī qāniyati ʼilīma

Hayyan ʻalāyu la-miphḫêmi
badê Ḫasisi miṣbatâmi

yiṣṣaqu kaspa yišlaḥu ḫarūṣa
yiṣṣaqu kaspa la-ʼalapīma
ḫarūṣa yiṣṣaqu-mi la-rababati

yiṣṣaqu ḫ-y-m wa-t-b-ṯ-ḫ
kitta ʼili dāta rabbatêmi
kitta ʼili nubbata ba-kaspi
š-m-r-g-t-ʼa baddī-mi ḫarūṣi

kaḥṯu ʼili naḫata ba-ẓāri
hudumu ʼil!i dū p-r-š-ʼa ba-b-ri

---

33. Note that the assembly of Byblos is called a *môʻēd* in the account of the journey of Wen-Amun of ca. 1100 B.C., *ANET*, p. 29, and John A. Wilson, "The Assembly of a Phoenician City," *JNES*, 4 (1945), 245. *Qubbah* in Num. 25 needs investigation as to whether it is a tent-shrine of a Canaanite deity.

naʿalu ʾili dū q-b-l-b-l
ʿalênna y-b-l-h-m ḫarūṣi

t̠ulḥanu ʾili dū malaʾa minī-mi
d-b-b-m dū masādati ʾarṣi

šuʿu ʾili d-qatu kī ʾamurri
s-k-natu kī ḥawwāti yamʾani
dū ba-hu raʾamūma la-rabbati

(4.1.20-44)

Here is something more
I would tell you. Present

Gifts to Lady Asherah of the Sea,
Presents to the Procreatrix of the gods.

Hayyan would go up to the bellows.
In the hands of Khasis, the tongs.

He would cast silver, beat out gold.
He would cast silver by the thousands (of shekels).
Gold he would cast by the myriad.

He would cast *hym* and *tbt̠h*.
A mighty dais of ten thousand (shekels),
A mighty dais . . . with silver,
. . . with poles of gold. (Exod. 25:13)

A mighty throne resting upon it.
A mighty footstool . . .

A luxurious couch (?) of . . .
Upon it . . . of gold.

An enormous table which is full of everything,
Of . . . of the foundations of the earth.

Gorgeous bowls with small animals shaped like wild
beasts of the Amurru,
Utensils shaped like the wild beasts of Yam'an,
Where are wild oxen by the myriads.[34]

The interpretation is not completely clear. Baal's messengers appear to be repeating Baal's instructions to Anat. It is necessary to have Asherah act as intercessor with El on behalf of Baal's temple. Only Asherah can bring about Koshar's working on the temple and its furnishings. The resulting description of Koshar making temple or palace furniture appears to be an elaborate "set piece." The use of *'il* in the description probably does not refer to El but means "mighty" or "pertaining to a god, divine," since the context is Baal's temple, not El's. Like similar descriptions of the metal worker and his marvelous craft in the *Iliad*, the poet has devoted much time and care to the description.

Is this description of the furnishings of a Canaanite temple of the second millennium another indication that the Israelite Tent of Meeting is a copy of a house or dwelling of the god? Many items in the desert tent,

---

34. The text bristles with difficulties. See Albright, *BASOR*, 91 (1943), 39-44; 93 (1944), 23-25; T. H. Gaster, *BASOR*, 93 (1944), 20-23; *BASOR*, 101 (1946), 21-30; *Thespis* (New York: Henry Schuman, 1950), p. 447, philological notes, as well as his translation and notes in the revised edition of *Thespis* (New York: Doubleday, 1961), pp. 173-174; H. L. Ginsberg, translation in *ANET*, p. 132.

like the furnishings just described, were cast *(yṣq)* of silver *(ksp)* and gold *(ẕhb)*. In both cases a divinely inspired craftsman did the work, Koshar and Bezalel. Although *kḥṯ* is not found in the Hebrew Bible, *h^a^dōm*, "footstool," in each of its six appearances in the Bible means the footstool of Yahweh. The verb *nûaḥ* is used in the Bible to describe the coming to rest of the Ark (and presumably of the Tent) in Num. 10:35:

> Arise, O Lord, and let thy enemies scatter and those that hate thee flee before thy face, and at its rest *(b^e^nūḥōt)*, let him say . . .[35]

Although there are not many direct connections between the Ugaritic text just cited and the Tent of Meeting, the descriptions of both are at home in the world of temple furnishings in the second and early first millennium in northwest Mesopotamia and Syria-Palestine.

If we recall that Israel spent a formative forty years in the southern area of Seir, Edom, Paran, Kadesh (and probably Sinai is best located here as well), where El the Warrior was apparently active, we are not surprised to find El characteristics in the religion of the "desert period."[36] The Arabic parallels to the Tent may

---

35. In Ps. 132:8, *qûmāh yhwh l^e^nûḥekā* (corrected according to 2 Chron. 6:41), "Arise, Yahweh, take thy (royal) seat," F. M. Cross, "The Divine Warrior," p. 22, n. 36.

36. The objection that the Ark and the Tent, according to the most ancient traditions, belong to the desert period and could therefore not be borrowed from the

well retain their validity. But it is probable that the Tabernacle/Tent of Meeting is a copy of the Tent of El.

Zion Traditions

According to 2 Samuel 5:7 (= 1 Chron. 11:5), the stronghold of Zion *(meṣūdat ṣîyôn)* was the earlier name of the city which David captured and named "The City of David." Zion occurs frequently thereafter as a designation of Jerusalem; Mount Zion is the ancient fortified hill between the Tyropoeon and Kidron valleys.

There are striking similarities between the mountain *ṣpn* in the Ugaritic texts and Mount Zion in the Hebrew Bible. On both, the deity dwells in his temple from which he exercises his rule; thunder and lightning are frequently his means of disclosure; the mountain is the scene of battle yet is impregnable; it is connected with fertility; and it is a cosmic center. This invites the question whether motifs of Zaphon, the residence of Canaanite Baal, have come to be associated with Zion, the residence of Yahweh.

Such a *translatio*[37] of motifs is a priori to be expected. Within the Ugaritic tablets themselves, there is

---

"sedentary civilizations of Canaan" is not valid. The highly sophisticated and urbanized people of Ugarit worshipped an El who lived in a tent! Israel came into contact with Canaanite civilization and religion in the "desert" period.

37. *Translatio* is a useful Latin ecclesiastical term which, among other meanings, describes the transference of the relics of a saint either from their original

a transfer of the battle between Anat (on behalf of Baal) and the dragon on Zaphon (3.3.34-4.48, esp. l. 45) to the heights of Lebanon.[38]

Many sacred mountains are attested in Canaan. Too little is known about them from archeology and from literary evidence, however (apart from Zaphon, Sinai, and Zion), to say with certainty that Zaphon traditions have been attracted to them. In the account of Philo Byblius of the history of culture (*Praep. Evang.* 10.6-14a), mountains play an important role. In what appears to be a sequence of old gods, sons of great size and stature are born whose names are applied to the mountains they occupied. The mountains are Mounts Zaphon *(tò kássios)*, Lebanon, Anti-Lebanon, and *tò brathú.*[39] From the giants

---

place of burial into an altar tomb or from one shrine to another. Both the original and the new shrine can sometimes be the repository of the same sacred tradition. For a brief introduction to the development of legends of Christian saints, and the transfer of the same motif from saint to saint and from place to place, see H. Delehaye, *The Legends of the Saints*, trans. V. M. Crawford (London: Longmans, Green & Co., 1907), esp. pp. 12-39.

38. The important lines are *tunn!āna lā-šabūma tašīt tirkas la-miryami laban*[*āni*], "she fixed the unmuzzled dragon, she bound him to the heights of Leban[on]." There is a fluidity of actors as well as of mountains. In 3.1.1-3 and probably in *PRU*, II, 1.1 (*RS* 15.134) *muḫ̮aṣu baʿlu . . . tunnāna*, "Baal killed . . . the dragon."

39. For *brathu* as Amanus, see W. F. Albright, *JBL*,

who bore mountain names were begotten Samemroumos, that is, Hypsuranios, and *Ousōos*.[40] If an old theogony is behind the confused account, then divinized mountains play a role in the structure of the cosmos.[41]

The deity Baal Hammon (= Mt. Amanus) in Phoenician and Punic inscriptions refers not to Baal Hadad but to

---

40 (1941), 211-212. O. Eissfeldt has identified *brathu* as Tabor, "Der Gott des Tabor und seine Verbreitung," *Archiv für Religionswissenschaft*, 38 (1934), 14-41.

40. The mountains are followed in the sequence by *Samēmroumos ho kai Hypsouranios kai Ousōos*. Hypsuranios is the Greek of *Samēmroumos*, "high heavens." *Ousōos* is *Ušu*, *Utu*, mainland Tyre in Egyptian and Akkadian texts. The *šmm rmm* in the Bodastart inscriptions (*KAI* 15), and the similar expression *šmm ʾdrm* (*KAI* 14.16, 17) in the Eshmunazor inscription, both of the fifth century (J. Brian Peckham, *The Development of the Late Phoenician Scripts* [Cambridge, Mass.: Harvard, 1968], p. 89, for date), appear to be temple precincts in Sidon around which the city or district is clustered. These precincts of the temple represent by their name and probably by their shape elements of the cosmos, in typical Ancient Near East religious fashion. The earthly city around these precincts is thus grounded in the eternal order. That similar ideas were operative in the Ugarit texts is shown by the name of Anat, *bʿlt šmm rmm*, "mistress of the high heavens." *Ugaritica*, V, 2.9 (*RS* 24.252, p. 551).

41. For a recent treatment of this section of Philo Byblius, see L. R. Clapham, "Sanchuniathon: The First Two Cycles" (unpub. diss., Harvard University, 1969), esp. p. 114.

Canaanite El.[42] The deity Baal Lebanon is known from a Phoenician inscription of between 774 and 738 B.C.,[43] but again it is impossible to say whether Baal Lebanon is Canaanite El or Baal and what is the deity's relation to the mountain. The same must be said of Baal Hermon, known from Judges 3:3 and 1 Chronicles 5:23 as a place name.[44] Mount Carmel was a sacred mountain from time immemorial, but what deity was resident upon it cannot be decided with certainty.[45] Mount Tabor is mentioned in

---

42. B. Landsberger, *Sam'al* (Ankara: 1948), pp. 45f, and Albright, *Yahweh and the Gods of Canaan*, pp. 233-234.

43. *KAI* 31 and Peckham, *Late Phoenician Scripts*, pp. 14-15.

44. A. Alt claims that a cult place on top of Hermon was a *Grenzheiligtum* between Aramaeans and Phoenicians, *ZDPV*, 70 (1954), 142-146. *Ḫermôn*, from its name, may have been connected to holy war.

45. Among the views: Baal in the Elijah episode (1 Kings 18) is a local god, to be distinguished from the god honored by Ahab and Jezebel, so A. Alt, "Das Gottessurteil auf dem Karmel," *Festschrift Georg Beer* (Stuttgart: W. Kohlhammer, 1935), pp. 1-18. Baal of Carmel is Baal Shamem, so Otto Eissfeldt, "*Ba'alšamēm* und Jahwe," *ZAW*, 57 (1939), 1-30. He is Melqart, R. de Vaux, "Les prophètes de Baal sur le Mont Carmel," *Bulletin du Musée de Beyrouth*, 5 (1941), 7-20; H. H. Rowley, "Elijah on Mount Carmel," *Bulletin of the John Rylands Library*, 43 (1960-61), 190-219. One ought to consider Baal Zaphon. The deity is mentioned in the treaty between Baal of Tyre and Esarhaddon, ca. 675 B.C. The contest concerns rain and fertility and the storm plays a central role.

several texts of the Old Testament as a sacred mountain (Ps. 89:13; Jer. 46:18; Hos. 5:1), but unfortunately, little information is conveyed about the deity worshipped there.[46] Mount Garizim is another mountain with some importance in Israel's religion. There the blessings were proclaimed in Deuteronomy 27. In Judges 9:37 and Ezekiel 38:12 occurs the phrase *ṭabbūr hā'āreṣ*, which the Septuagint translates as *omphalos tēs gēs*, "navel of the earth."[47]

Although this investigation of Canaanite sacred mountains (outside of Ugaritic and the Hebrew Bible) has yielded little, there is firmer ground with regard to a site in the northeast Egyptian Delta. *Ba'al Ṣᵉpôn* is one of the stations on the route of the Israelite Exodus (Exod. 14:2, 9; Num. 33:7). Otto Eissfeldt in 1932 showed successfully that Baal Zaphon in the Egyptian Delta was also called *Zeus Kasios* in Greek and that both reflect *b'l ṣpn* at home near the city of Ugarit.[48] It is

---

46. Bibliography and discussion in H. J. Kraus, *Worship in Israel*, trans. G. Busell (Richmond, Va.: John Knox, 1966), pp. 165-172.

47. The usage in Judg. 9:37 seems nonmythical. There may be a mythic overtone in Ezek. 38, yet its isolated use makes it impossible to say much further. See Walther Zimmerli, *Ezechiel*, BK XIII (Neukirchen: Verlag des Erziehungsverein, 1969), pp. 955-957 for full discussion.

48. *Baal Zaphon, Zeus Casios und der Durchzug der Israeliten durchs Meer* (Halle: Niemeyer, 1932), to be supplemented by W. F. Albright, "Baal-Zephon," *Festschrift*

now possible to identify Baal Zaphon in Egypt precisely thanks to a letter found at Saqqara, *l bʿl ṣpn w l kl ʾl tḥpnḥs*, "to Baal Zaphon and every god of Tahpanhes" (*KAI* 50.2-3). Tahpanhes is a city in the northeast Delta and is identical with Greek Daphne (derived from *ṣpn*), today called Tell Defneh. According to Herodotus (III.5), Typhon, the Greek monster, is buried there. One ancient version in Greek mythology tells of the fight between Zeus and Typhon, fought on Mount Casios.[49] The connection of Typhon with Egyptian Mount Zaphon-Casios, and the finding of a grave stone with the personal name *Casios* from Roman times, along with a Nabatean inscription with the mention of *Zeus Kasios* (= Baal Zaphon), make it clear that Baal and his mountain have been "translated" from Syria.[50]

In the Old Testament, Zaphon is the name of a city of Gad (Josh. 13:27). It appears in Egyptian records of the nineteenth dynasty as *Ḏapuna*. In an Amarna letter it is *Ṣapuna* and the residence of a princess known as the "lady of the lions.[51] It has been identified as Tell

---

Alfred Bertholet (Tübingen: J. C. B. Mohr, 1950), pp. 1-14.

49. Typhon was not finally vanquished on Casios, Apollodorus, I. 40; Nonnos, Dionys., I, 154f., II. Cited and commented upon by H. J. Rose, *A Handbook of Greek Mythology*, 6th ed. (London: Dutton, 1958), p. 59.

50. Eissfeldt, *Baal Zaphon*, pp. 40-41. The spread of Baal Zaphon even further afield is shown by the fourth century Marseilles Tarif, *KAI* 69.1.

51. The existence of the town of Zaphon is well established from the Late Bronze Age to the period of the

el-Qoš on the north side of the Wadi Rajid,[52] and with Tell es-Sa'idiyeh on the Wadi Kufrinjey, north of Succoth.[53] We can infer that Zaphon here is a "translation" from the mountain in North Syria. Like the location of Baal Zaphon in the Egyptian Delta, the myth complex probably became attached to the site.

A clearer indication of the transfer of motifs from Zaphon to a hill within Israel is provided in Exodus 15.[54]

Maccabees. W. F. Albright, *Yahweh and the Gods of Canaan*, p. 122, n. 29.

52. Wright-Filson, *Westminster Historical Atlas to the Bible*, 2nd ed. (Philadelphia: Westminster, 1956), p. 128.

53. Y. Aharoni, *The Land of the Bible* (Philadelphia: Westminster, 1967), p. 31, and W. F. Albright, *Yahweh and the Gods of Canaan*, p. 122, n. 29.

54. Ps. 68:16-17 may refer to one sacred mountain being replaced by another:

> O mountain of God (or mighty mountain), Mount Bashan,
> O many-peaked (?) mountain, Mount Bashan,
> Why do you look with envy (?)
> O many-peaked (?) mountain,
> At the mountain God desired for his dwelling,
> Yea, there Yahweh will dwell forever.

The precise interpretation of the verses is hindered by uncertainties of translation, particularly of the root, *rṣd*, "to envy" (?). E. Douglas van Buren has collected glyptic evidence showing gods, dressed in scales representing mountains, bowing before other mountain gods. On one seal, the Weather-god strides over the mountains and

Baal describes his own mountain dwelling, *ba-tôki ǵūriya ʾili ṣapāni/ba-qudši ba-ǵūri naḥlatiya/ba-naʿami ba-gibʿi talʾiyati* (3.3.26-28), "in the midst of my mountain, godly Zaphon,/in the holy place, the mountain of my heritage,/in the chosen spot, on the hill of victory." The dwelling of both Mot (4.8.12-14; 5.2.15-16) and Koshar (1.3.2, restored; 3.6.15-16) is said to be *kissiʾu ṯibtihu/ʾarṣu naḥlati*, "the throne where he sits/the land of his heritage." The same language is found toward the end of Exodus 15:

16ʿad yaʿabōr ʿammeka yhwh
ʿad yaʿabōr ʿam zû qānîtā
tebiʾēmô wetiṭṭaʿēmô
behar naḥalātkā
mākôn lešibtekā
pāʿaltā yhwh
miqdāš yhwh
kônenû yādeykā
18yhwh yimlōk
leʿōlām wāʿed

When thy people passed over, Yahweh,
When thy people passed over whom thou hast created,
Thou didst bring them, thou didst plant them

---

pulls down a prostrate deity by grasping the top of his horned cap. In front of the conquering god, a third divinity emerges from the highest of the three mountains. He raises his right hand in salutation and on his left arm carries a hare to present to the higher god. "Mountain Gods," *Orientalia*, 12 (1943), 79-80.

In the mount of thy heritage,
The dais of thy throne
Which thou hast made, Yahweh,
The sanctuary, Yahweh,
Which thy hands created.
Yahweh will reign
Forever and ever![55]

The usual interpretation of the "mount of thy heritage" is the mountain of the Temple in Jerusalem, and in later times this was indeed how the verse was understood. Yet the poem is too early to have depicted originally Israelite Mount Zion.[56] The "mount of heritage" must have originally meant the hill country of Canaan as Yahweh's special heritage. The sanctuary *(miqdāš)* founded by Yahweh is the earthly representation of the temple-palace of the god. It was probably at Gilgal.[57] Here, then, is another instance of the traditions of Zaphon attaching themselves to mountains in the land of Israel.

---

55. For a recent treatment of this song and its Canaanite background, see F. M. Cross, "The Song of the Sea and Canaanite Myth," *Journal for Theology and the Church*, 5 (1968), 1-25. Cross's translation on pp. 15-16 is used here.

56. Ibid., pp. 9-12, for the evidence for a late 12th or 11th century date.

57. The "mountain" need not be a lofty peak. A temple precinct in Sidon was termed "the high heavens!" And little Mount Zion was to be exalted as the tallest of the mountains (Isa. 2:2 = Mic. 4:1). See Cross, ibid., p. 24.

If traditions of the high gods of Canaan, El and Baal, associated themselves with venerable mountain peaks all over Syria-Palestine, then it is only to be expected that Mount Zion, the center of Israelite piety from the time of David, would attract traditions common to the religion of Canaan.[58] Yahweh's borrowing of characteristics of Canaanite El is well known.[59] Equally to be reckoned with, especially in regard to Zion traditions, is the borrowing of Baal language and traditions. Zion in Psalm 48 is explicitly called Zaphon, the name of Baal's mountain. Just when the mixing of the language and traditions connected with the two gods El and Baal took place is difficult to say. Did it take place in the cult of pre-Israelite Jerusalem? Did Canaanite El, who apparently was worshipped in southern Canaan, retain his ancient role as a warrior god, and thus receive "Baal language"?[60] It can only be said that in the Ugaritic myths El and Baal are clearly distinguished, though their

---

58. For discussion with bibliography of the much-debated question of the pre-Israelite cult of Jerusalem, see H. J. Kraus, *Worship in Israel*, pp. 179-236. Also Gunther Wanke, *Die Zionstheologie der Korachiten*, BZAW, 97 (Berlin: Alfred Töpelmann, 1966), esp. pp. 70-117.

59. Among the many discussions, F. M. Cross, "Yahweh and the God of the Patriarchs," esp. pp. 232-259; Patrick D. Miller, "El the Warrior," pp. 411-431.

60. For discussion of the mixing of El and Baal traditions, see Werner H. Schmidt, *Königtum Gottes in Ugarit und Israel*, 2nd ed., BZAW, 80 (Berlin: Alfred Töpelmann, 1966), pp. 55-58.

relationship is not clearly defined. The Phoenician inscriptions show that the Canaanite pantheon is fluid and has local variations. The Patriarchs seem to be dealing with Canaanite El, judging by the names of the deities they encounter. By the time of the earliest Israelite poetry, for example, the Song of the Sea (Exod. 15), Yahweh is described in Baal language--the motif of the battle with the sea and probably the mount of heritage, the fruit of the victory over the sea, clearly belong to the Baal tradition. Yet the Sinai traditions, in the main, are El traditions.

Allowing, then, for some mixture of Baal and El language in descriptions of Yahweh, we now turn more explicitly to Zion. Serving occasionally as the Israelite reflex of Zaphon, it naturally is the focus of Baal language. In the Hebrew Bible, Zion occurs mostly as the name of Jerusalem *qua* religious center. In some uses, however, Zion is no mere geographical designation but bears a meaning enriched by mythical motifs. The clearer instances of the mythically heightened uses will be discussed. Discussion will be confined chiefly to the Psalms and First Isaiah.

In the Psalms, "Zion" is taken up into the cult language and used often. A number of different contexts of Zion in the Psalms can be discerned: kingship and inviolability of Zion over against the nations; site of the Lord's presence; simply a synonym of Jerusalem; place of liturgical worship; goal of restoration after the exile; place which the Lord has chosen; city which the Lord has founded. The contexts are not necessarily mutually exclusive.

Under the heading of the inviolability of the city,[61] there are some particularly instructive passages.

> 2Great is Yahweh,
> And greatly to be praised,
> In the City of our God,
> His Holy Mountain *(har qodšō)*,
> 3The Beautiful Height *(y^e^pēh nôp)*,
> The Joy *(m^e^śôś)* of the whole earth,
> Mount Zion,
> The Reaches of Zaphon *(yark^e^tê ṣāpôn)*,
> The City of the Great King.
> 4Yahweh is in her citadel,
> Has shown himself her bulwark.
> 5Indeed, the kings assembled,
> Together they raged.
> 6They gazed, yea, they were astounded.
> The were in panic, they fled.
> 7Trembling took hold of them,
> Anguish as of a woman about to give birth,
> 8As *(k^e^!)* the east wind
> Shatters the Tarshish ships.
>
> (Ps. 48:2-8)

The glorification of the city of God (vv. 2-4) is by depiction of an attack by enemy kings *(Völkersturm)* and their defeat (vv. 5-8). There follows the acknowledgment

---

61. The obscure saying of the inhabitants of Jebusite Jerusalem, when David comes to attack, "You will not come in here, but the blind and the lame will drive you away" (2 Sam. 5:6) may be a reference to belief in the inviolability of Jerusalem.

of Yahweh's power (vv. 9-12). Verses 13-15 are to be interpreted as a call to procession. The psalm belongs to the class of "Songs of Zion."[62]

In this psalm, the complex of Zaphon traditions known from Ugarit appear clearly. The descriptive phrases, "City of our God," "His Holy Mountain," "The Beautiful Height," "The Joy of the whole earth," "Mount Zion," "The Reaches of Zaphon," "The City of the Great King," all are in apposition, and some are clearly related to the description of the mountain dwellings of the gods in Ugaritic.[63] These descriptive phrases, some Canaanite in origin, are now applied to Mount Zion, the mountain of Yahweh.

Not only are epithets of Canaanite mountain dwellings of gods applied to Zion in the Psalter. Attacks upon the mountain by enemies of God are attested both in the Psalter (Pss. 2, 46, 48, and 76) and in the

---

62. H. J. Kraus, *Psalmen*, BK XV (Neukirchen: Verlag des Erziehungsverein, 1960), p. 356.

63. *Har* is the semantic equivalent in Hebrew to Ugaritic *ǵr*, both being regularly paired with *gbʿ(h)*, "hill." *Ǵr* is the regular Ugaritic word for the mountain of Baal. Hebrew *yᵉpēh* could be the semantic equivalent to Ugaritic *nʿm*, both being used of the beauty of women and of sacred mountains (*CTA* 3.3.28). *Yarkᵉtê ṣāpôn* seems to be equivalent to Ugaritic *ṣrrt ṣpn*, so M. Dahood, *Psalms I*, Anchor Bible (Garden City, N.Y.: Doubleday, 1965), pp. 289-290. *Mlk rb*, "great king," is the Ugaritic equivalent of Akkadian *šarru rabû*, "the suzerain, the great king."

Ugaritic texts (3.3.34-4.48, especially 44-45 and 4.7.25-27).

Gunther Wanke has recently insisted on the intra-Israelite origin of the *Völkerkampf*, the motif of the kings raging helplessly against the mountain of God. He derives it from the "enemy from the north" passages in Jeremiah. In postexilic times, the motif was applied to Jerusalem, and the psalms with this motif are accordingly postexilic.[64] The Ugaritic texts, which Wanke does not exploit sufficiently, show us that the *Völkerkampf* is no isolated motif but is found in Canaanite religious literature of the second millennium as part of the tradition complex of the holy mountain dwelling of Baal. We should therefore see verses 2-3 and verses 4-8a of Psalm 48 as a single unit. The holy mountain dwelling of God (vv. 2-3) is impregnable (vv. 4-8a).

Baal's mountain was attacked but the attackers were driven away. Anat, recalling her fight against the monsters who attacked Baal, asks rhetorically

ʼimtaḫisa kaspa ʼittariṯa ḫarūṣa
ṭāridi ba‘la ba-miryami ṣapāni
m-š-ṣ-ṣ (?) k‘(ṣ/l) (?) ʼudnāhu
gārišihu la-kissiʼi mulkihu
la-n-ḫati la-kaḥṯi darkatihu

(3.3.43-4.47)

Did I not wrest the silver, plunder the gold

---

64. *Die Zionstheologie der* ***Korachiten***, pp. 73-92. R. de Vaux, on other grounds, has criticized Wanke's dating of the Korahite psalms to postexilic times in "Jerusalem et les prophètes," *RB*, 73 (1966), 508-509.

Of the one(s) who would drive Baal from the heights
of Zaphon,

. . . . .

Of the one(s) who would expel him from his royal
throne,
From the dais, from his powerful seat?

The entire passage, *CTA* 3.3.34-4.48, ought to be compared since it tells of other combats of Anat (and Baal) against various monsters, perhaps some of the battles taking place at Zaphon. In another passage from the Baal cycle, Baal celebrates his kingship in thunder and lightning, scattering enemies in fright from his holy mountain.

yiptaḥu ḥallāna ba-bahatīma
'arubbata ba-qirba hēkalīma
yiptaḥu ba'lu bidqāti 'ar-pāti
qālahu qaduši ba'lu yattinu
yaṯniyu ba'lu ṣi'ta šapatêhu
qālahu qa[duši]r 'arṣu
. . . ǵūrīma
taḫūšūna raḥāqu . . .
. . . qadmu yammi
bamātu 'arṣi taṭṭutna
'ibū ba'li ti'hadu ya'arīma
šāni'ū Haddi g-p-ti ǵūri
wa-ya'ni 'al'iyānu ba lu
'ibū Haddi t(?) lama tāḫūšu
lama tāḫūšu nāṯiqū dāmirāna
'ênu ba'li qaddima yadahu
kī taǵḏī 'arzu ba-yamīnihu
ba-kī-mā yāṯibu ba'lu la-bahatīhu

ʾu milku ʾu bal-milku
ʾarṣa darkati yištakinu (?)
d-l-la ʾal ʾilʾaka la-bini ʾili-mi Môti
ʿ-d-d la-yadidi ʾili ǵāziri
(4.7.25-47)

He opened a window in the temple,
A casement in the midst of the palace.
Baal opened clefts in the clouds.
Baal uttered his holy voice.
Baal discharged the utterance of his lips.
His holy voice . . . the earth.
. . . the mountains.
The distant . . . were quaking . . . (?)
. . . sea.
The high places of the earth tottered.
The enemies of Hadad took to the wooded heights.
The haters of Hadad, to the . . . of the mountain.
And Aliyan Baal said,
"Enemies of Haddu, why are you quaking?
Why are you quaking, attackers of the Valiant One?"
The eye of Baal anticipated his hand,
When . . . the cedar (club) in his right hand.
Indeed, Baal is enthroned in his temple.
"No king or commoner,
A land of sovereignty shall establish.
Tribute (?) I will not send to the son of El, Mot
Gifts of homage (?) to the beloved of El, Ghazir.[65]

---

65. *Philological notes: t!ḫsn.* In place of *ʾaḫ̮šn*

Cosmic upheaval is associated closely with the attacks of Baal's enemies. Baal's victory-thunders shake

---

of the copy read *tḫšn*. In ll. 38-39, Herdner in *CTA* incorrectly has *tḥš* for *tḫš* of the copy and photograph. Aistleitner confuses the two roots *ḥs* and *ḫs*, and translates both as "to hasten, to flee," *Wörterbuch der Ugaritischen Sprache*, 3rd ed., O. Eissfeldt, ed. (Berlin: Akademie-verlag, 1967), no. 1093. (Hereafter abbreviated as *WUS*.) *Ḥš* in *ḥš bhtm k[ṯr] ḥš rmm hk[lm] ḥš bhtm tbn[n] ḥš trmm hk[lm]*, "Quckly, O Koshar, houses; quickly erect palaces; quickly let houses be built, quickly let the palaces be erected!: is best taken as "to hasten." The cognates are Hebrew *ḥûš* I (// *mhr*), possibly related to Akkadian *ḫâšu*, "to hasten," despite the different laryngal. See Moshe Held, "The Action-Result (Factative-Passive) Sequence of Identical Verbs in Biblical Hebrew and Ugaritic," *JBL*, 84 (1965), 273, and n. 26, and W. von Soden, "Akkadisch *ḫâšum* 'sich sorgen' und Hebraisch *ḥuš* II," *Ugarit Forschungen*, I (Neukirchen: Kevelaer, 1969), 197. *Ḫs* therefore does not mean "to hasten." In the absence of satisfactory etymologies and cognates, context alone must be relied on. Something akin to "to quake" is indicated.

nṯq. Its parallelism with *ʾib* suggests a relation with Hebrew *nešeq*, "weapons." The Hebrew verb *nāšaq* appears to be a later denominative from the noun. "(Armed) attacker" seems appropriate.

dmrn. Herdner in *CTA* wrongly *dmrm*. As an epithet of Baal, *dmrn* occurs here and in *PRU*, V, 1 reverse 8 (19.39) in an obscure context. Umberto Cassuto has

the high places of the earth. Now that Baal's kingship is established by the decree of El, and by the building

---

suggested that Zeus Demarus of Philo Byblius (*Praep. Evang.*, 1.10.18-19; 28; 31) is Ugaritic (Baal) *dmrn*, most recently in *The Goddess Anath* (Jerusalem: Bialik, 1965), p. 46. Otto Eissfeldt, "Adrammelek und Demarus," *Annuaire de l'Institut de Philologie et d'Histoire Orientales et Slaves*, 13 (1953), 153-159, repr. in *KS*, III (Tübingen: J. C. B. Mohr, 1966), 335-339, although not excluding Cassuto's suggestion, prefers associating Zeus Demarus with the name of the river *Nahr ed-Damur* (p. 336). I would suggest that *dmrn* is a variant of *ḏmr*, with the *-ānu* ending, "the one of." There can be an interchange of *d* and *ḏ* in Ugaritic; see Gordon, *UT*, p. 26, sec. 5.3. *Ḏmr* in Ugaritic is "sentry, soldier," and the root occurs in Hebrew, *zmr*, as "protector, defense," Amorite *zmr*, "to protect," and in the proper name *Zimri-Addu*. For further references, see Walter Baumgartner, *Hebräisches und Aramäisches Lexikon zum Alten Testament* (Leiden: Brill, 1967), p. 263, *sub voce zmr* III and proper name *zimrî*. If this suggestion is valid, we could translate tentatively, "the Valiant One."

ktǵḏ. Aistleitner's adducing of Arabic *ǵušiya*, "to fall into powerlessness," and Akkadian *ḫašu*, "be covered, be darkened, be weak" (*WUS*, no. 2176) are phonetically unlikely. M. H. Pope suggests as possible cognates Arabic **ǵss*,,"plunge, dip," or *ǵaḏḏa* in IV stem, "accelerate, hasten," in Paul L. Watson, "Mot, the God of Death, at Ugarit and in the Old Testament" (unpub. diss. Yale University, 1970), p. 37.

of the palace (with its window), the enemies (or enemy) of Baal are put to rout. The enemies are not specified but they surely include Mot who in the following verses summons Baal to the underworld.[66]

Psalm 46 is another psalm which tells of the glory of Zion in mythic terms.

> 2 Yahweh[67] is our shelter and our stronghold.
> 3 As help in trouble he is well proved.
> Therefore we will not fear when the earth totters (?),
> And when the mountains topple into the midst of the seas.
> 4 Though its waters roar and foam,
> Though the mountains quake before its boiling up.
> . . . . .[68]

---

66. One other Ugaritic text on inviolability of a city from profane attack is 14.3.133-136. King Pbl tells Krt not to attack his city because *ʾudumu yatūnatu ʾili/ wa-ʾušānu ʾabī ʾadami*, "Udum is a gift of El, and a donation of the Father of Man."

In the light of the Ugaritic parallel to the storming of God's mountain, it is possible to be more exact than Kraus who sees "eine historisierende Variante zu dem urzeitlichen Chaoskampf der Weltentstehungsmythen." *Psalmen*, p. 358.

67. In the Elohistic part of the Psalter, "Yahweh" is the more original reading than "Elohim."

68. MT *nāhār pelāgāyw yeśammeḥû ʿîr ʾelōhîm qedōš miškenê ʿelyôn*, literally, "river, its streams make glad the city of God, holiness of the tents of the Most High." The Septuagint takes *qdš* as a Piel, "The streams of the

6 Yahweh is in her midst;
She shall not be moved.
Yahweh will help her
At the break of dawn.
7 The nations rage, the kingdoms totter,
He utters his voice, the earth melts.
8 Yahweh of hosts is with us.
Our stronghold is the God of Hosts.
9 Come, see the works of Yahweh
Who has made destruction in the earth.
10 He makes wars to cease to the ends of the earth.
The bow he breaks, and the spear he shatters.
The wagons he burns with fire.
11 Be still and know that I am God.
I am exalted among the nations.
I am exalted in the earth.
12 Yahweh of Hosts is with us.
Our stronghold is the God of Jacob.

---

river make glad the city of God; the Most High sanctifies his tents." The most serious objection to the usual translation, "There is a river whose streams make glad the city of God," is the context. Verses 3-4 speak of threatening waters and chaos. One would expect *nāhār* "river" to continue the theme of threatening water chaos. Dahood has seen the problem and has boldly corrected:

Though its waters rage and foam,
the mountains heave in its midst,
the river and its channels stand in a heap.
God brings happiness to his city,
the Most High sanctifies his habitation.

(Psalms I, p. 277)

Textual problems make it uncertain whether a stream arises in Zion, the city of God. As in Psalm 48, the turmoil of nature is connected with the enemy attacks on God's city. Yahweh's thunders proclaim his victory. He destroys the weapons of the enemy who have tried to storm the sacred place.[69]

Psalm 76, another *Zionlied*, speaks of Yahweh's tent[70] on Zion. Zion is the place where the weapons of "the kings of the earth" are broken before the superior power of God defending his dwelling on Zion (v. 13; cf. Pss. 2:2, 10; 48:4).

> 2 Yahweh is known in Judah.
> In Israel, great is his name.
> 3 His tent was in Salem,
> And his dwelling, in Zion.

---

69. One would like to compare *CTA* 3.3.11-14, *qryy b'arṣ mlḥmt št b'prm ddym sk šlm lkbd 'arṣ 'arbdd lkbd šdm*, which is the message Baal and, on another occasion, El (*CTA* 1.2), send to Anat. The details are not clear, but apparently victory has been won and Anat is to cease warring and become her other self, the goddess of fertility.

70. That *sukkô // meʿônātô* of v. 3 mean "tent // dwelling," or the like, is indicated by Ps. 27:4-5. The Psalmist speaks of dwelling in the house *(bêt)* of the Lord and of inquiring in his Temple *(hêkālô)*, and in the same breath says, "He will hide me in his *sukkōh* in the evil day. // He will hide me in the shelter of his tent *('ōhalô)*. // He will set me on a high rock." See H. J. Kraus, *Psalmen*, p. 526.

[4]There he shattered the flashing arrows,
Shield and sword and weapons of war.

The rest of the psalm, which is in a somewhat damaged state, speaks of the defeat of God's enemies and of his judgment.

In Psalm 2, however, we have the clearest instance of the *Völkerkampf* in the entire psalter.

[1]Why do the nations gather
And the peoples plot vain things?
[2]Why do the kings of the earth take their stand,
And the princes take counsel together
Against Yahweh and against his anointed?
[3]"Let us break their bonds
And throw off their yoke from us."
[4]The Enthroned in heaven laughs
The Lord makes sport of them.
[5]Then he will say to them in his wrath,
And terrify them in his anger.
[6]"But I have anointed my king
Upon Zion, my holy mountain."
[7]And I will recite the decree of Yahweh.
"He said to me, 'You are my son,
Today I have begotten you.'"

Enemy kings rage against Yahweh and Yahweh's king. Yahweh, enthroned in the heavens, laughs in scorn and announces he has anointed his king and placed him on the holy mountain. Then another person tells of the decree *(ḥōq)* which has established the human king and given him power over earthly sovereigns. In the Ugaritic passage just quoted, Baal derides his enemies in similar fashion,

"Enemies of Haddu, why are you quaking?/Why are you quaking, attackers of the Valiant One?" (4.7.38-39). Several passages attest the massing of Baal's enemies against Zaphon (3.3.34-4.48; 4.7.35-45; 5.1) and their defeat.[71] The nations and the ends of the earth are to be the *nḥlt* and the *ʾḥzt* of the Israelite king (v. 8), recalling the land or mountain of heritage of the god in Canaanite religion.

In the Israelite adaptation of the *Völkerkampf* against the holy mountain in some psalms, Zion has replaced Zaphon. Unspecified earthly kings act out on the earthly plane the assaults against Zaphon in the heavenly sphere. The breaking up of the weapons of war on the holy mountain, it may be assumed, is the earthly reflection of the victory over those who would assault the heavenly Zaphon. Yahweh, however, unlike Baal, is not a seasonal deity who suffers periodic defeat by Mot. His mountain is therefore impregnable and becomes a symbol of the secure place.[72]

---

71. The bonds and cords of Ps. 2:3, of which the kings speak, may be related to the muzzling of the dragon by Anat in 3.3.37, *lā ʾištabimu tannīna*, "Did I not muzzle *(šbm)* the dragon?" When the myths about the kingship of the deities is transposed to the earthly sphere, earthly kings and princes tend to replace the more mythical monster of the myths. There was a terrestrial plane to the heavenly myths. Also, the *ḥōq*, decree, that establishes the king recalls the *tḥm* of El granting kingship to Baal.

72. Isa. 25:6-8 tells of the victory feast of Yahweh after his victory over Death *(Môt)* on the mountain,

Not only were motifs of Zaphon pressed into service to glorify Mount Zion, the residence of Yahweh. Some psalms appear deliberately to invoke the Sinai traditions of revelation in storm. This theophany language, at home in the traditions of Mount Sinai, was utilized in the Jerusalem cultus to impress upon the worshipper that the God of Sinai reveals himself anew on Mount Zion. Israel in the Temple liturgy relives the primal experience of Yahweh at Mount Sinai.

Psalm 50, a prophetic liturgy of judgment, is a good example of this tendency. In the "March in the South" passage, Deuteronomy 33:2, "Yahweh came forth from Sinai./He beamed forth from Seir upon us./He shone forth *(hôpîʿ)* from the mountain country of Paran," Yahweh is pictured as coming in a stately procession from the southern mountains to aid his people in holy war. In Psalm 50:

> 1 The God of Gods, Yahweh,
> Spoke and summoned the earth
> From the rising of the sun to its setting.
> 2 From Zion, the perfection of beauty,
> Yahweh shone forth *(hôpîʿ)*.
> 3 Our God comes and will not be silent,
> Before him is a devouring fire,
> Round about him a raging tempest.
> 4 He summoned the heavens above,
> And the earth to the trial of his people.

Just as Yahweh shone forth *(hôpîʿ)* from Sinai as he

---

as in *CTA* 6.6. Unlike Canaanite myth, Mot will not rise after his defeat. He has been depersonalized in Isa. 25.

came to the aid of his people, so now he shines forth *(hôpîʿ)* from Zion to judge his people.

In Psalm 18 (= 2 Samuel 22), an archaic royal song of thanksgiving, Yahweh rescues his favored one in a storm theophany similar to that of Sinai in Exodus 19. Again, in Psalm 97, Yahweh comes as vindicator in a storm. The cult of the Jerusalem Temple celebrates the coming of the One of Sinai to his people in Zion-Jerusalem. These psalms affirm the identity of the God of Mount Sinai and the Law with the God of Zion.

In 2 Kings 18:13-20:19 (= Isaiah 36:1-39:8), which tell of Hezekiah and the Assyrian attack, is revealed how the belief in Zion's inviolability had mixed itself into the political life of the nation. Isaiah, in the face of the enormous and hostile Assyrian power, counsels hope, for the Lord will defend the city to save it. The dogma of the inviolability of Zion recurs frequently in the preaching of Isaiah of Jerusalem though in tension with his word of judgment against Jerusalem.[73]

Many passages in Isaiah tell of the inviolability of Zion, in particular 29:1-8; 31:1-6.[74] It is impossible

---

73. A good discussion of this tension in Isaiah's preaching can be found in Gerhard von Rad, *Old Testament Theology*, trans. D. M. G. Stalker (New York: Harper, 1962), II, 155-169.

74. John H. Hayes, "The Traditions of Zion's Inviolability," *JBL*, 82 (1963), 419-426, sees as special Zion themes of Pss. 46, 48, and 76 taken up in Isaiah: Isa. 10:5-11, 27b-34; 14:24-27, 28-32; 17:12-13; 28:14-22; 29:1-8; 30:27-33; 31:1-8; 33:20-24.

to decide with certainty whether these passages have their roots in pre-Israelite traditions, though given the relation of the Isaian passages on Zion to the Zion passages in the psalms, it may be assumed that they do.

There is one passage in Isaiah that appears to have mythical features indicating Canaanite origin:

In the latter days,
Established shall be the mountain of the house of
    Yahweh.
At the head of the mountains ⟨it shall be high⟩[75]
And it will be higher than the hills.
And all the nations shall flow to it.
And many people will come and say,
"Come, and let us go up to the mountain of Yahweh,
To the house of the God of Jacob,
That he may teach us his ways,
And we may walk in his paths."
Surely from Zion shall come forth the Law,
And the word of Yahweh from Jerusalem.
And he shall judge between the nations,
And shall decide for many peoples.
And they shall beat their swords into plowshares,
And their spears into pruning hooks.
Nation shall not take up sword against nation,
Neither shall they learn war any more.

(Isa. 2:2-4; = Mic. 4:1-3)

---

75. Father John Kselman, S.S., suggests in a forthcoming article that *rām* has been omitted by haplography. For collocation of *rm* and *nśʾ*, see Isa. 57:15.

Whatever the date or authorship of the passage, the intent of the passage is clear.[76] Tiny Mount Zion is to tower over the other mountains.[77] Yahweh's wisdom is not confined to Jerusalem, but will go forth to the whole world. Yahweh as ruler on his mountain will put a stop to all wars. The proverb to turn plowshares to swords and pruning hooks to spears, which probably originated in mustering peasants in time of war, is reversed.[78] With Yahweh effectively ruling on his mountain, over the nations, there will be no need for men to fight. As in Psalms 46 and 48, the weapons of war are destroyed at the foot of the holy mountain. Mount Zion remains inviolable. The holy mountain is appropriately the place from where the authoritative word goes out. We have seen above that the theophany and law-giving of Sinai was renewed in the

---

76. The Micah authorship of this passage is now largely abandoned and it is generally attributed to Isaiah. For a recent defense of Isaian authorship and a review of opinions, see Hans Wildberger, *Jesaja*, BK X (Neukirchen: Verlag des Erziehungsverein, 1965), p. 80.

77. "At the head of the mountains," *b*^{e}*rôʾš̌ hehārîm*, does not mean the highest point of a peak but the position at the head of a range of mountains, as Arnold Ehrlich pointed out many years ago in his *Randglossen zur Hebräischen Bibel* (Hildesheim, 1968 repr. of 1912 edition), IV, 10. See n. 54 above where it is suggested that Ps. 68:16-17 may refer to mountains honoring a greater mountain. Such a reference may be in the Isaian passage as well.

78. Wildberger, *Jesaja*, p. 87.

Jerusalem cult. The logical outcome was to see Zion as the place from which the Law went forth.

Another passage from Isaiah, 33:20-22, introduces us to a theme that recurs in Ezekiel 47:1-12, Zechariah 14:8, and Joel 4:18 (E. VV. 3.18), the river flowing from the holy mountain.

> 20 Look upon Zion, the city of our festivals,
> Let your eyes look upon Jerusalem,
> A quiet encampment, an immovable tent.
> Its stakes will never be plucked up,
> And none of its cords will be broken.
> 21 But there mighty Yahweh will be for us
> A place of broad rivers.[79]
> No galley with oars can go there,
> Nor stately ship can pass.
> 22 For the Lord is our judge, the Lord is our ruler,
> The Lord is our king, he will save.

The verses, whether from Isaiah or some later hand, describe the Tent of Meeting, the predecessor of the Temple, which had disappeared centuries before. The suspicion is, therefore, that ancient tradition of the Tent of El at the source of the waters is reproduced here. If this be so, we have another glimpse at the Canaanite tradition behind the dogma of the inviolability of Zion.

In Joel 4:18 (E. VV. 3.18), in Zecharaiah 14:8, and especially in Ezekiel 47:1-12 dealing with the future of Jerusalem, life-giving waters issue from the holy mountain to the surrounding territory. No spring ever

---

79. *Nehārîm* appears to be a gloss.

existed in the Temple of Jerusalem, at least not a spring of the volume of water described. The detail is deliberately introduced to show that the New Temple will not be a self-enclosed entity but will bring blessing and life for the surrounding land. The fact that in Ezekiel the Temple is located "upon a very high mountain" (40:2)[80] invites the question whether the abode of El at the source of the streams in the Ugaritic texts is behind the scene. In the Ugaritic texts which describe the dwelling of El, El's dwelling is at the "sources of the Two Rivers, in the midst of the pools of the Double-Deep." In Genesis 2:6, the *ʾēd* rises from the earth to water the whole face of the land. The *ʾēd* is in all probability Akkadian *idu*, "river," as has been seen. In verses 10-14 of the same chapter, a river *(nāhār)* arises in Eden to water the garden. The river then divides into four streams, the Tigris, the Euphrates, the Gihon, and the Pishon. In Ezekiel 28, Eden is located on the mountain of God, but the association of Eden and mountain of God appears to be late. However, there does seem to be a general relation between the passages--paradise, the dwelling of God, garden and/or mountain, as the source of life-giving waters.[81]

---

80. The "very high mountain" has upon it a structure "like the structure of a city *(kᵉmibnēh ʿîr)*. The fact that the mountain is not immediately identified as Zion nor the city as Jerusalem, when taken with Ezekiel's obsession with the presence of the Lord in these chapters, indicates that a mythic motif is present.

81. Otto Kaiser, *Die mythische Bedeutung des Meeres*, pp. 107-112.

These passages cannot be directly related to the holy mountain of El and Baal from Ugaritic myths, yet they do fit into the general picture of the holy mountain as a source of rain and fertility and even of order in the universe.[82]

In the instances of the Zion motif outside of the psalms and Isaiah, the same Zion traditions are used. Zion is a sacred mountain, inviolable by reason of Yahweh's choice of it as his dwelling place, a place of victory in war (particularly in Joel). The Canaanite roots in some of these passages can be discerned, though now the Yahwistic faith has transformed them. The Lord's dwelling with his people is contingent upon the people's faith and the Lord's total freedom. The mountain and city will be inviolable as long as its inhabitants have faith in the sovereign Lord who protects those who call upon him.

Archaic Traditions Other than Those Concerning Zion

Isaiah 14:10b-15, which is part of the longer passage

---

82. We should mention "the waters of Shiloah which flow gently" of Isa. 8:6, as possibly belonging to the same world view. In Gen. 2:13, the river Gihon is one of the four rivers that arise in the Garden. The Gihon is the river of Jerusalem and it may be intended to link paradise and the mountain, source of water, with Zion. Paradisiacal features of Zion are clear in Ezek. 28. Possibly Isa. 11:9, "They shall not hurt or destroy in all my holy mountain," takes up the theme of Yahweh's victory over his enemies on the mountain.

14:4b-21, preserves ancient Canaanite lore of a holy mountain.

You have become weak like us.
You have become like unto us.
Your pride is brought down to Sheol,
The sound of your harps.
Maggots are the bed beneath you,
And worms are your covering.
How are you fallen from heaven,
Helel ben Shahar!
How are you felled to earth,
Conqueror of the nations (?)![83]
And you said in heart,
"I will ascend to heaven
Above the stars of El.[84]
I will set my throne on high, I will sit enthroned
On the mount of the (divine) council.
On the recesses of Zaphon,[85]

---

83. The phrase is parallel to Helel ben Shahar and possibly a misunderstood divine epithet of Helel, or perhaps it is *Šalimu* who is also met in *CTA* 23.

84. Marvin H. Pope, *EUT* (Leiden: Brill, 1955), translates *kôk^{e}bê ʾēl* as "the highest stars." W. F. Albright understands the phrase as the circumpolar stars, "the far northern stars which never set," *Yahweh and the Gods of Canaan*, p. 232, and n. 69. They are to be identified with the members of the divine assembly. The "morning stars" of Job 38:7 are parallel to the sons of God.

85. In our interpretation, Zaphon is not parallel to the mount of assembly. Zaphon, parallel to *bām^{a}tê*

I will go up upon the high clouds.
I will become like Elyon!"
But you are brought down to Sheol,
The recesses of the Pit.

Preserved here is one of the several fragmentary references in Ugaritic and the Hebrew Bible to the revolt in the heavens. Genesis 2-3 and Ezekiel 28, as well as *CTA* 6.1 and 23, give a tantalizing glimpse of a rebellion against the chief god of the pantheon. The full story behind the references, and the relation of them to the battles for supremacy in the Canaanite pantheon preserved in Greek writers, Hittite sources, and Philo Byblius, is impossible now to reconstruct.[86]

ʿāb, "the backs of the clouds, the high clouds," seems on the way to the use of Zaphon in Job 26:7:

nōṭeh ṣāpôn ʿal tōhû
tōleh ʾereṣ ʿal bᵉlî-māh

(Yahweh) stretching Zaphon over the void,
Suspending the earth on nothing (?)

Zaphon's meaning seems to be practically "heavens." *Nōṭeh* elsewhere is used of "heavens" in the Old Testament and it forms a reasonable merism with *ʾereṣ* in the passage from Job. It is easy to imagine the development of the meaning of Zaphon, under Israelite impulse, from "mountain (dwelling of God)" to "heavens (dwelling of God)." See further H. L. Ginsberg, "Reflexes of Sargon in Isaiah after 715 B.C.," *JAOS*, 88 (1968), 51.

86. P. Grelot sees parallels to the fall of Phaeton in Greek mythology as well as to the Ashtar myth of Ugarit

A Ugaritic text which tells of an attempt to take over the throne of Baal is given here for comparison.

tiššaʼu gāha wa-taṣūḥu
tišmaḫa hitta ʼaṯiratu wa-banūha
ʼilatu wa-ṣabbūratu ʼaryīhu
kī mita ʼalʼiyānu baʻlu
kī ḫaliqa zubūlu baʻlu ʼarṣi
gômā yaṣūḥu ʼilu
la-rabbati ʼaṯirati yammi
šumʻī la rabbatu ʼaṯiratu yammi
tinī ʼaḥada ba-banīka ʼamallikannu
wa-taʻni rabbatu ʼaṯiratu yammi
bal namallika Yadiʻ Yalḥan
wa-yaʻni luṭpānu ʼilu dū pāʼidi
daqqu ʼanīmi la yarūẓu ʻim baʻli
lā yaʻdubu m-rḥa ʻim bini dagani kī t-m-s-m
wa-ʻanā rabbatu ʼaṯiratu yammi
biltu namallika ʻaṯtara ʻarīẓa
yamluka ʻaṯtaru ʻarīẓu
ʼappinnaka
ʻaṯtaru ʻarīẓu yaʻli ba-ṣrrt ṣapāni
yaṯibu la-kaḥṯi ʼalʼiyāna baʻli
paʻnāhu lā tamǵiyāni huduma
riʼšuhu lā yamǵiyu ʼapsahu
wa-yaʻni ʻaṯtaru ʻarīẓu
lā ʼamluka ba-ṣrrt ṣapāni
yaridu ʻaṯtaru ʻarīẓu
yaridu la-kaḥṯi ʼalʼiyāna baʻli

---

in "Isaiae xiv 12-15 et son arrière-plan mythologique," *RHR*, 149 (156), 18-48.

wa-yamluk ba-arṣi ʼili kulluhu

(6.1.39-65)

She (Anat) lifted her voice and cried,
"Let Asherah and her sons rejoice,
The goddess and her brood of young lions.
For dead is Aliyan Baal,
For departed is the Prince, Lord of the Earth."
Loudly El cried out,
To Lady Asherah of the Sea,
"Hear, O Lady Asherah of the Sea,
Give one of your sons; I will make him king."
And answered Lady Asherah of the Sea,
"Let us make Yadi-Yalhan (= "Understanding One"?)[87] king."
And Benign El, the Kindly One, said,
"Too weak, he cannot compete with Baal in a race,
Cannot hurl a spear with the Son of Dagan when they contend with one another.(?)"
And Lady Asherah of the Sea said,
"Let us make Ashtar the Rebel king.
Let Ashtar the Rebel be king!"
Thereupon
Ashtar the Rebel went up to the reaches of Zaphon.
He sits enthroned on the throne of Aliyan Baal.

---

87. *Ydʿylḥn*. Elephantine Aramaic *lḥn*, "temple servant," may be a cognate, thus literally, "he knows how to serve," i.e., he will be obsequious or at least more docile than Ashtar. Or Arabic *laḥina*, "to understand, be intelligent," offers good contrast to the physical might and toughness of Ashtar.

His feet did not reach the footstool,
His head did not reach the top.
And Ashtar the Rebel said,
"I will not reign on the reaches of Zaphon."
Ashtar the Rebel came down,
He came down from the throne of Aliyan Baal.
And he reigned over the whole of the vast earth.

One may conjecture that in variants of the myth in Ugaritic violence might come more to the surface (Ashtar is after all described as violent), but in this version the focus is on the conflict between Baal and Mot, not on the conflict between Baal and Ashtar or El and Ashtar. Ashtar and his brothers are here rather lifeless pawns on the side of Mot and his mother.

In *CTA* 23, *Šaḥru*, "Dawn Light," is paired with *Šalimu*, "Evening Light," that is, they were the Morning-star and the Evening-star. Thus they are apparently the hypostases of Ashtar as Venus. It is another indication of the single story ultimately behind both Isaiah 14 and *CTA* 6.1, yet also of the variants of the story. *Šaḥar* in Isaiah 14:12 is the father of the rebel god *Hēlēl*.

In the Ugaritic text, Baal has been found dead, a victim of Mot. Anat, after mourning him, buries him on Zaphon. She then comes to El at the source of the Two Rivers, the source of the Double-Deep, and cries out in anguish. A son of Asherah is to take Baal's throne. Asherah nominates Yadiyalhan. El, the old king-maker, rejects him because he cannot match Baal's physical prowess. The second nominee, Ashtar, has the physical strength but not the stature to take Baal's place. He is the first to see it and steps down and reigns over the earth, evidently leaving the mountain of Baal and the power to control the heavenly waters which give fertility.

These gods are not rivals to El but to Baal. There is no conflict. El simply refuses to designate one nominee king while the other disqualifies himself.

The difficult and enigmatic text, "The Beautiful and Gracious Gods" (*CTA* 23) may refer to the rebellious god(s). The first part of the text which is rubrical, designates a particular area (perhaps near or in the temple--a counterpart of a heavenly area) as the "field of El," *šadu ’ili*.

yalittā ’ilêmi naʻamêmi
’ag-r-y-n banê yômi
yāniqê-mi ba-’appê ḏadê šitti
šapatu la-’arṣi šapatu la-šamīma
wa-ʻarābu ba-pîhumā
ʻiṣṣurū šamīma wa-dagū ba-yammi
wa-nadāda gazirā la-<g>azri
yuʻdubu ’u yamīnu ’u šam’ālu ba-pîhumā
wa-lā tišbaʻāni
ya ’aṯṯatā ’itraḫu
ya banā ’ašallidu
ša’a ʻ-d-b tôk midbari Qadiši
ṯamma tagagirā la-’abanīma wa-la-ʻiṣṣīma
šabʻa šanāti tammāti
ṯamāne naqapāti
ʻad ’ilāmi naʻamāmi
titallikāmi šada
taṣūdāni pi’ata midbari
wa-nagāšu humā nāġira midraʻi
wa-ṣūḥa humā im nāġiri midraʻi

ya nāǵiru nāǵiru pitaḥ
wa-patāḥu huwa pirṣa ba‹adihumā
wa-‘arābu humā
himma [’ êṯa--? la]ḥmu wa-ti[nā wa-nilḥam
himma ’êṯa[--? yênu wa-]tinā wa-našti
wa-‘anā humā nāǵiru midra‘i [’eṯa laḥmu. . .]
’eṯa yênu

(23.60-74)

They (the two wives of El) have borne the beautiful
gods,
. . . the day-old ones,
Sucking the dugs of the breasts of the Lady.
One lip to earth, one lip to heaven.
And there entered into their mouths
The birds of heaven and the fishes of the sea.
And they ran from bite to bite.
Both right and left were set in their mouth
And they were not satisfied. (Cf. Isa. 9:19)
"O wives I have married!
O sons I have begot!"
Lift . . . in the midst of the Desert of Qadesh.
They sojourned amid stones and trees,
Seven whole years,
Eight cycles;
While the beautiful gods
Walked about the steppe.
They traversed the confines of the wilderness.
And they approached the guard of the sown land.
And they cried out to the guard of the sown land.
"O guard, guard, open!"
And he opened a breach behind them,

And they entered.
"If there is . . . bread, give that we may eat.
If there is . . . wine, give that we may drink."
And the guard of the sown land said to them, ["There is bread]
There is wine."

Šaḥru and *Šalimu* are the names of the two sons of El (line 52). The two young gods are put out to pasture, but their voracious appetites make it necessary for them to go to more fruitful surroundings, where there is plenty of food and wine. A guard lets them in and feeds them. One could conjecture that these two gods are rebel gods, breaking into the "field of El," which was mentioned earlier in the text. The two gods would then be rebelling against El. In *CTA* 6.1., Ashtar tried to take the kingship on Zaphon which was rightfully Baal's. Here *Šaḥru*, seemingly another name for Ashtar, may be breaking into the paradisiacal field of El. In Ezekiel 28, the paradise of El is seen as the holy mountain.

Whatever may be the validity of these observations on the Ugaritic texts, Isaiah 14 clearly tells of an unsuccessful assault by Helel ben Shahar on the seat of El himself. The upstart deity wants to be enthroned over the divine assembly on El's mountain. He wants to be on the recesses of Zaphon, reigning on the backs of the clouds. Zaphon is not necessarily synonymous with the mount of assembly. Ashtar also was to exercise his kingship on the heights of Zaphon (6.1.57). The passage is not, therefore, necessarily an instance of mixing of El and Baal language.

In Ezekiel 28 are contained two poems, verses 1-10 and verses 11-19, which, if not Canaanite in origin, make use of ancient myth.[88] In the first poem, verses 1-10, partly reprinted below, the prophet makes the Prince of Tyre lay claim to the office of El[89] and to El's dwelling[90] in the midst of the seas.

The phrase *b^e^lēb yammîm*, "in the heart of the seas," well describes the island situation of Tyre. It also may be an allusion to the dwelling of Canaanite El. The Ugaritic texts picture messengers going to El.

---

88. The two units have been redacted into one and concluded by v. 19b. In understanding Ezekiel, one must take into account the history of the text which has been expanded and commented upon by a kind of Ezekielian "school." For detailed treatment, consult the recent and thorough commentary of Walther Zimmerli, *Ezechiel*, BK XII (Neukirchen: Verlag des Erziehungsverein, 1969).

89. For the most recent discussion whether *ʾēl* should be translated "El," the Canaanite god, or "God," see H. J. van Dijk, *Ezekiel's Prophecy on Tyre* (Rome: Pontifical Biblical Institute, 1968), pp. 95-96. Though the prophet understands *ʾēl* as "God," the original subject was Canaanite El, as the other allusions to Canaanite myth in the two poems (and elsewhere in Ezekiel) indicate. In the Ugaritic myths, however, the two pretenders are after the throne of Baal while El is the unthreatened arbiter (*CTA* 6.1).

90. H. J. van Dijk, *Ezekiel's Prophecy on Tyre*, insists that *môšab ʾelōhîm* is "the seat of a god" or "a divine seat" (pp. 97-98). The more obvious parallel is the *mṯb ʾil* in the Ugaritic texts where El dwells with his court. See Chap. III, n. 36.

ʿim ʾili mabbikī naharêmi
qirba ʾapīqī tihāmātêmi

(3.5.13-16; 4.4.20-24; 6.1.32-36; 2.3(?).4-5; 17.6.46-49)

Toward El at the sources of the Two Rivers,
In the midst of the pools of the Double-Deep.

The phrase *beləb yam* or *bᵉlēb yammîn* seems in some usages in the Hebrew Bible to be a maritime term, "the high seas" (Prov. 30:19; Ezek. 27:25,26,27). In other texts, however, the cosmic sea beneath the earth is meant (Exod. 15:8; Ps. 46:3; Job 2:4 *bilbab yammîm*). The primary meaning of the phrase in Ezekiel 28:2 in its present state appears to be the island of Tyre. That it originally designated the location of El's abode is indicated by other features of Canaanite myth, the revolt in the heavens, the stress on wisdom which is a characteristic of El, the anomalous use of *ʾēl* (in Ezekiel, only here and v. 9). In short, *bᵉlēb yammîm* appears to be the Hebrew equivalent of Ugaritic *qrb ʾapq thmtm*.[91]

---

91. *Yammim* in the Hebrew Bible can be paired with *nᵉharot* in Ps. 24:2 or *nāhār* in Jon.22:4 as Ugaritic *thmtm* and *ym* can be paired with *nhr(m)*. *Qrb* in Ugaritic is semantically equivalent to *lēb* in Hebrew. Both Hebrew and Ugaritic use organs of the middle of the body for "in the midst of," e.g., *beṭen, lēb, kabid, qirbu*. In *CTA* 11.1, *qrb* means "female sexual organs."

Zimmerli, understanding El's dwelling to be a place of banishment in the underworld, denies that "heart of the seas" refers to El's dwelling. Living in banishment would not be something to aspire to (*Ezechiel*, p. 668).

Of verses 1-10, verse 2 is the most relevant for our purposes.

ya‘an gābah libbekā
watō’mer ’ēl ’ānî
môšab ’ĕlōhîm yašabtî
belēb yammîm
we’attāh ’ādām welō ’ēl
watittēn libbekā kelēb ’elōhîm

Because your heart has become proud
And you have said, "I am El.
(In) the dwelling of El I sit enthroned,
In the heart of the seas."
But you are a man and not El,
Though you regard your wisdom as the wisdom of El.

The Canaanite background of the dwelling of El is discernible in these verses, though now all is used to construct a word of judgment against the Prince of Tyre.

The second poem, verses 11-19, is difficult textually and shows that expansion by disciples of Ezekiel so characteristic of the book that bears the prophet's name.

You . . .
Full of wisdom and perfect in beauty,
You were in Eden, the garden of God.
Every precious stone was your defense (?).[92]
Carnelian, topaz, and jaspar,
Sapphire, carbuncle, and emerald.

---

92. Cf. Mic. 7:4 where *mesûkāh* means "fence, hedge." See van Dijk, *Ezekiel's Prophecy on Tyre*, pp. 116-117.

. . . .

On the holy mountain of God you were,
In the midst of the stones of fire you walked.
You were perfect in all your ways
From the day of your creation,
Until iniquity was found in you.
In the abundance of your trade
You have filled yourself[93] with violence and you
sinned.
And I will cast you as a profane thing from the
mountain of God,
And I will drive you out, O guardian cherub (?)
From the midst of the stone of fire.

(vv. 12b-16)

Despite many textual problems, it is clear that the second poem tells of rebellion against the Canaanite god. To the rebel is again ascribed wisdom. He lives in Eden which is the mountain of El.[94] He walked as a trusted

---

93. Reading *mallô* for MT *mālû*, the infinitive absolute with the value of a perfect form. Van Dijk, *Ezekiel's Prophecy on Tyre*, p. 121.

94. It is not certain that there is a clear identification between "the garden of God" and "the holy mountain of God." The passage appears not to have been composed at one time but expanded by disciples. Zimmerli thinks the "garden of Eden" is not part of the *Grundtext* but an anticipation of "cherub" in v. 14 (*Ezechiel*, pp. 678-679). It is the only instance in the Hebrew Bible where the concept of the garden of God and that of the holy mountain of God have been unmistakably associated.

member of the heavenly court until iniquity (complicity in a palace intrigue?) was found in him. The "stones of fire" may well be the equivalent of the "stars of El" of Isaiah 14:13--both perhaps the *banū ʾili*, "the sons of El," considered from an astral point of view.[95]

Both Ezekiel and Isaiah, as well as Ugaritic texts, suggest conflicts on the mountain--all of them conflicts regarding kingship. The texts of Isaiah 14 and Ezekiel 28 seem to tell of rebellion against El in his paradisiacal garden, on his holy mountain. They may be related to the theomachies preserved in Hesiod, Hittite sources, and Sanchuniathon.

The Book of Ezekiel contains the strange narrative of the invasion of the holy land and ultimately the destruction of the chief prince Gog of Meshech and Tubal (38.1-39.29). The geographical allusions, and the possible mythological background, have intrigued commentators for centuries.[96]

> 38:1-9. [1]And the word of the Lord came to me, saying, [2]"Set thy face against Gog, the chief prince of Meshech and Tubal and prophesy against him [3]and say, 'Thus has Yahweh spoken. See, I am against you, Gog

---

95. For a review of the many interpretations of *ʾabnê ʾēš*, see Zimmerli, *Ezechiel*, pp. 685-686. In Job 38:7, the *kôkᵉbê bōqer*, "the morning stars," are parallel to *bᵉnê ʾelohîm*, "the sons of God."

96. For a judicious and detailed treatment of the entire Gog pericope, see Zimmerli, *Ezechiel*, pp. 921-975. Zimmerli's analysis of primary and secondary material has been followed in the translation.

chief prince of Meshech and Tubal, [4]and I will bring you forth and all your army, horses and horsemen, all of them clothed in full armor, a great company--many people are with you. [7]Be ready and keep ready, you and all the hosts that are assembled about you, and be a guard for them. [8]After many days you will be mustered; in the latter days you will go against the land that is restored from war, the land where people were gathered from many nations upon the mountains of Israel which had been a continual waste. Its people were brought out from the nations and they all dwell securely. [9]And you will go up like a storm, you will advance like a cloud to cover the land.'"

39:1-5. [1]And you, son of man, prophesy against Gog, and say, "Behold, I am against you, Gog, chief prince of Meshech and Tubal, [2]and I will turn you about and drive you forward, and bring you up from the uttermost parts of the north, and lead you against the mountains of Israel; [3]then I will strike your bow from your left hand, and will make your arrows drop out of your right hand. [4]You shall fall upon the mountains of Israel, you and all your hordes and the peoples that are with you; I will give you to birds of prey of every sort and to the wild beasts to be devoured. You shall fall in the open field; for I have spoken, says the Lord."

39:17-20. [17]As for you, son of man, thus says the Lord, "Speak to the birds of every sort and to all beasts of the field, 'Assemble and come, gather from all sides to the sacrificial feast which I am

> preparing for you, a great sacrificial feast upon the mountains of Israel, and you shall eat flesh and drink blood. [18]You shall eat the flesh of the mighty, and drink the blood of the princes of the earth--of rams, of lambs, of goats, of bulls, all of them fatlings of Bashan. [19]And you shall eat fat till you are filled, and drink blood till you are drunk, at the sacrificial feast which I am preparing for you. [20]And you shall be filled at my table with horses and riders, with mighty men and all kinds of warriors,'" says the Lord.[97]

Walther Zimmerli has isolated the oldest stratum of the text thus: 38:1-9 (with some additions), 39:1-5, 17-20. Traditio-historical analysis separates out three traditions, one arising from the "enemy from the north" motif such as is found in Jeremiah, another from passages from Isaiah containing the *Zionstheologie*,[98] and the third, the sacrificial meal which Yahweh himself prepares.

Are the latter two motifs, the annihilation of the enemy on the "mountains of Israel" and the sacrifice offered there reflections of Canaanite myth? On Mount Zaphon Baal fights and defeats his enemies. In 39:9-10 occurs the motif of destroyed weapons. According to Psalms 46, 48, and 76 this takes place on Mount Zion.

---

97. The *Grundtext*, as established by Zimmerli, eliminates 38.4a, c; 5; 6a, b; 9c; 10-23; 39.6-16; 21-29.

98. Zimmerli sees the strongly emphasized proclamation of the annihilation of the enemy on the mountains of Israel (38:8; 39:2, 4, 17) as deriving remotely from the *Zionstheologie* of Isaiah, e.g., Isa. 14:24f (pp. 939-940).

Both these motifs seem distant from the Ugaritic myths, but one must allow for the possibility of a reflex of the myth in the Gog pericope.

For the sacrificial feast upon the mountains[99] which Yahweh gives, there is no parallel in what remains of Canaanite religion.[100] The gods give feasts on mountains in Ugaritic literature only to greet and to honor another god or to celebrate the erection of a temple. The motif of the slaughter does have an intra-Israelite parallel, however (Isa. 34:5-8). It has been suggested by H. Gressmann and Sigmund Mowinckel that the feast on the mountain of the bodies of the enemy is a transformation of the eschatological picture of the "joyous feast,"[101] such as we find in Isaiah 25:6-8. The feast on the mountain celebrating the erection of the palace and the dynamic kingship of God has roots in Canaanite mythology (*CTA*

---

99. The introduction of the birds and the beasts seems to reflect the same traditions as are found in Jer. 12:9 and Isa. 56:9. "Mountains of Israel" in Ezekiel is the whole land and is synonymous with *ʾadmat yiśrāʾēl*, "the land of Israel." Zimmerli, *Ezechiel*, p. 147.

100. In a Ugaritic text, the body of Mot may be eaten by birds in 6.2.35-37, but the scene does not take place on a mountain.

101. H. Gressmann, *Der Ursprung der israelitisch-jüdischen Eschatologie* (Göttingen: Vanderhoeck and Ruprecht, 1905), p. 141, and Sigmund Mowinckel, *Psalmenstudien II. Das Thronbesteigungsfest Jahwes und der Ursprung der Eschatologie* (Amsterdam: P. Schippers, 1961, repr. of 1921-24), p. 296f; Zimmerli, *Ezechiel*, p. 953.

6.6). In Isaiah 25:6-8, God destroys death at the same time he offers the joyous victory banquet. Possibly, the banquet for the victorious on the mountain and the slaughter-sacrifice of the enemies are one and the same--the celebration of the life and the kingship of the deity on the mountain site of his temple.

Cosmic-Mountain Symbolism in the Solomonic Temple

Among the Canaanites, the high god was thought to dwell in a temple or tent on the holy mountain. The earthly temple of the deity was considered a copy of the heavenly temple on the mountain. This earthly-heavenly correspondence can be illustrated, for example, from the temple of Baal excavated in Ras Shamra[102] and from the precincts of *šmm rmm*, "highest heaven," and *šmm ʾdrm* "mighty heavens," in the temple of Sidon.[103] Israelite religion, too, saw a correspondence between the heavenly prototype and its earthly copy, for example, the institution of holy war when the heavenly army marches with the earthly army (Judg. 4:14 and 2 Sam. 5:24), and the Priestly theology of the Sabbath where (at least in Gen. 1) the Sabbath imitated a divine pattern.

The Solomonic Temple reflects similar correspondence, though the interpretation of individual elements in the Temple remains difficult. In Psalm 48, the phrases of verses 1-3, "his holy mountain," "the city of the great kind," and so on apply both to the mountain of Yahweh and to Mount Zion. The Tent of Meeting, the

102. See above, Chap. III, n. 28.

103. See above, Chap. III, n. 40.

predecessor of the Temple, is the earthly copy of the heavenly Tent of Meeting of the Divine Assembly of Canaanite religion.[104] The Israelites were careful, of course, to make distinctions between God enthroned in his dwelling in heaven and his Name which is in the Temple, as in Solomon's prayer in 1 Kings 8.

Some scholars, building on the thesis that there is a correspondence between the heavenly and the earthly temple, have tried to see cosmic symbolism in some of the furnishings of the Solomonic Temple--the pillars Jachin and Boaz in front of the Temple, the Bronze Sea in the court, the laver *(kîyôr)*, and the Ezekielian altar of burnt offering.[105] Without further specific evidence, these suggestions must remain conjectural. It is likely, however, that individual elements of the Solomonic Temple are cosmic in the sense that they represent elements of the temple in the heavens.[106]

---

104. R. J. Clifford, "The Tent of El and the Israelite Tent of Meeting," *CBQ*, 33 (1971), 221-227.

105. W. F. Albright, *Archaeology and the Religion of Israel*, 3rd ed. (Baltimore: Johns Hopkins, 1953), pp. 142-155. In the fifth ed., Anchor Paperback (Garden City, N.Y.: Doubleday, 1969), there has been no change in Albright's position. Also see G. E. Wright, *Biblical Archaeology*, 2nd ed. (Philadelphia: Westminster, 1962), pp. 137-146.

106. For a generally skeptical view of cosmic symbolism in the Solomonic Temple, see de Vaux, *Ancient Israel*, pp. 328-330. De Vaux, however, understands "cosmic" as reflecting the cosmos, rather than reflecting the heavenly temple, the sense of cosmic in this section.

There are difficulties if one understands the cosmic symbolism of the Temple as related to the cosmos, that is, reflections of the structure of the universe. The Temple is cosmic in the sense that the Temple of Jerusalem represents the true Temple which is the source of order in the world. Albright has assembled the evidence that the pillars in the front of the Temple were cosmic in the sense that they were related to the structure of the universe.[107] More evidence is needed as well as a clearer understanding of the meaning of cosmic in this context. The Bronze Sea *(yam)* has the best possibility of being cosmic in significance because of the conflict which appears occasionally in the Bible between the deity and the sea.[108] In Ezekiel 43:13-17, the altar of burnt offering is built in three square stages. The base *(ḥêq hā'āreṣ)* is taken most naturally as an architectural term related to *ḥêq* of 1 Kings 22:35, the inside of a chariot. It is probably not "the bosom of the earth." The *ha'ᵃri'êl*, the top of the altar, remains unexplained. We have no way of knowing if the Israelites saw it as the

---

107. Albright, *Archaeology and the Religion of Israel*, pp. 144-148. For a recent review of theories on Jachin and Boaz, see W. Kornfeld, "Der Symbolismus der Tempelsäulen," *ZAW*, 74 (1962), 50-57. Recently, Jean Oulette has suggested that the pillars are part of the temple structure and related to the Mesopotamian *bīt hilâni*, "Le Vestibule du Temple de Salomon etait-il un *Bīt Hilâni*?" *RB*, 76 (1969), 365-378.

108. For a recent treatment of the Bronze Sea with bibliography, see H. J. Kraus, *Worship in Israel*, p. 187.

har ʾēl, "mountain of God." The laver *(kîyôr)* seems not to have cosmic significance.[109]

In summary of the theme of the cosmic mountain in the Hebrew Bible, it can be said that the mountains are a prominent feature of the geography and the religion of Israel. Many of the prominent heights were sacred places before the formation of Israel, and they remained so during her history. The two great holy mountains in Israel were Sinai and Zion. Difficulties standing in the way of calling them "cosmic mountains" have been noted. The term is rooted in a particular view of the sacred mountains which is not fully verified in Israel and Canaan. Sinai, though, quite clearly stands in the tradition of holy mountains in Canaan where decree and revelation are uppermost, where the deity seems to dwell in a tent. It is similar, therefore, to the traditions regarding Canaanite El as they are known from the Ugaritic texts. The traditions surrounding Zaphon of Baal seem to have

---

109. Beside being a laver of copper, *kîyôr* is said to have designated a platform as well in 2 Chron. 6:12-13 and to have had cosmic symbolism, being derived from Sumerian *ki-ùr* which can have the meaning "foundation of the earth" in a cosmic sense. So Albright, *Archaeology and the Religion of Israel*, pp. 152-154. However, Hebrew *kîyôr* is cognate to Akkadian *kiuru*, "metal basin," while another, different Akkadian word, *kiūru* (from Urartian *gi(u)ra*), means "surface of the earth." So A. Salonen, *Die Hausgeräte der alten Mesopotamien* (Helsinki, 1965), p. 267, n. 1, and W. von Soden, *Akkadisches Handwörterbuch* (Wiesbaden: Harrassowitz, 1965), p. 496.

adhered to various sacred mountains all along the Levant--Lebanon, Zion, and Tahpenhes in the Egyptian Delta. Baal takes possession of mountain, temple-palace, and kingship after he has won it by battle and been appointed by El. With his enemies fallen, and enthroned upon his holy mountain, he proclaims his power in thunder and lightning. These themes were put to good use in Zion where Yahweh's eternal (not periodic) kingship was celebrated. Elements of both Baal and El traditions are found very early in Israel--Baal elements from the Zaphon traditions and El elements from the Sinai traditions and from the traditions connected with the Canaanite shrines. The Solomonic Temple cannot be proved in its individual elements to have reflected the cosmos or structure of the universe, but it undoubtedly reflected the heavenly temple. Allusions to a revolt against the high god are preserved here and there in the Hebrew Bible, but only in a most fragmentary way.

IV. THE COSMIC MOUNTAIN IN INTERTESTAMENTAL LITERATURE

With the Babylonian Captivity and the resulting development of Jewish communities outside of Palestine, Jerusalem the holy city came to play a large role in the religious imagination of Jews.[1] Mount Zion as a cosmic mountain of the type found in the early Canaanite and Hebrew literature, however, does not appear in our sources. In the period when source material is fairly abundant, from about 200 B.C. to A.D. 100, Jerusalem and Mount Zion are portrayed in language and motifs drawn from the earlier classical era. Yet there has been a change. Jerusalem remains a center, to be sure, but now in a horizontal, geographical sense. In Enoch's journeys (1 En. 17-19 and 21-36), Jerusalem is not the place of divine-human intersection where divine power is operative on the earthly plane, as it is in some classical Old Testament passages. Rather it is the midpoint of Enoch's legendary

---

1. For bibliography, see K. L. Schmidt, "Jerusalem als Urbild und Abbild," *Eranos Jahrbuch*, vol. 18, ed. Olga Fröbe-Kapteyn (Zurich: Rhein Verlag, 1950), pp. 207-248, and J. H. Seeligmann, "Jerusalem in Jewish-Hellenistic Thought," *Judah and Jerusalem*, The Twelfth Annual Archeological Convention (Jerusalem: Israel Exploration Society, 1957), pp. 192-208 (in Hebrew).

travels. For continuation of the old sacred mountain motifs in a living form, we must go to some traditions of Mount Hermon at the sources of the Jordan River.

The Septuagint, the Greek translation of the mid-third century B.C., translates the Hebrew *ṭabbūr hā'āreṣ* in Judges 9:37 and Ezekiel 38:12 as *omphalos tēs gēs*, "navel of the earth." *Ṭabbūr* in Judges 9:37 simply means a height. The Ezekelian usage may mean "center of the earth" in the context of mythic geography such as is found in 1 Enoch, discussed below. The usage is similar to *omphalos*, "navel," applied to the shrine of Delphi in Greece.[2]

A representative passage portraying Jerusalem as the center in this sense in legendary geography is 1 Enoch 26:1-5. Enoch has traveled to the west, to the places of punishment of the angels and to the seven mountains of the northwest. He comes upon Jerusalem as he heads east.

> And I went from thence to the middle of the earth, and I saw a blessed place in which there were trees with branches abiding and blooming of a dismembered tree. And there I saw a holy mountain, and underneath the mountain to the east there was a stream and it flowed towards the south. And I saw towards the east another mountain higher than this, and between

---

2. Samuel Terrien, "The Omphalos Myth and Hebrew Religion," *VT*, 20 (1970), 315-338, provides an extensive bibliography. See also Wilhelm Caspari, "ṭabur (Nabel)," *ZDMG*, NS 11 (1933), 49-65, and Zimmerli, *Ezechiel*, BK XIII (Neukirchen: Verlag des Erziehungsverein, 1969), *ad* 38.12.

> them a deep and narrow ravine: in it also ran a stream underneath the mountain, lower than the former and of small elevation, and a ravine deep and dry between them: and another deep and dry ravine was at the extremities of the three mountains. And all the ravines were deep and narrow, (being formed) of hard rock, and trees were not planted upon them.[3]

Enoch leaves the mountain-garden throne of God in the northwest (chaps. 24-25) and comes to the blessed place in the middle of the earth. Though the name is not used, the place is Jerusalem. After the description of Jerusalem, he makes a journey to the east, evidently intended to balance his journey to the west. The centerpiece of the two journeys is Jerusalem, in the middle of the earth. The geographically accurate, nonmythic description of Jerusalem shows that "middle of the earth" is not a point which joins heaven and earth. "And there I saw a holy mountain and underneath the mountain to the east there was a stream and it flowed toward the south" (1 En. 26:2). This is a perfectly straightforward description of the actual stream issuing from the foot of Mount Zion. The stream does not issue from the Temple as it does in the descriptions of Ezekiel 47:1-12 and Joel 3:18 (E. VV. 4.18) and Letter of Aristeas 89, or with the fantastic volume of Zechariah 14:8. Jerusalem is in the middle of the earth because it is the halfway point in

---

3. All translations, unless noted, are from R. H. Charles, *The Apocrypha and Pseudepigrapha of the Old Testament in English*, vol. II (Oxford: Clarendon, 1913).

Enoch's second journey (chaps. 21-36) from the west to the east.[4]

The motif of battle at the sacred mountain is a common one in the Canaanite texts and in the classical Old Testament texts. The vestiges of the motif may occur in several passages from Enoch. In the Dream Visions (1 En. 83-90), the destruction of Israel's enemies will be followed by the resurrection and the coming of the messianic age. The judgment of the rebellious angels is portrayed vividly.

> And the judgement was held first over the stars, and they were judged and found guilty, and went to the place of condemnation, and they were cast into an abyss, full of fire and flaming, and full of pillars of fire. And those seventy shepherds were judged and found guilty, and they were cast into that fiery abyss. And I saw at that time how a like abyss was opened in the midst of the earth, full of fire, and they brought those blinded sheep, and they were all judged and found guilty and cast into this fiery

---

4. "Middle of the earth" sometimes describes simply the choice portion of land, as in Jubilees 8:12, 19; Sibylline Oracles, 5:250, and Testament of Naphtali, 8:1. Mountains appear in the fabulous geography of 1 En. 17:1-8; 18:6-19:3; 24:1-25:6. Even though old clichés appear in their description, precious stones, the mouths of all the rivers of the earth and the mouth of the deep, they appear to be only clichés and do not continue a live tradition.

> abyss, and they burned; now this abyss was to the right of that house. (1 En. 90:24-26)

Though the mythic character is manifest, the place of punishment is clearly Gehenna, west of Mount Zion and the Temple, "that house." Then the old Temple is removed and a new Temple is built at the center of the restored community. In 1 Enoch 18:19-19:3, the stars are punished near the base of the mountain. In 1 Enoch 27, in the mythically heightened description of Enoch's second journey, judgment is also exercised in the valley of Gehenna, to the west of the Temple. The righteous look on the fall of their foes, which is a frequent theme in the Old Testament. The history of Gehenna in passages of judgment such as these is easy to trace. Gehenna, or the valley of Hinnom, in earlier times the site of infant sacrifice by fire, came to be seen as the place of fiery punishment of the unjust. Mount Zion had come to be seen as the abode of the just.[5]

Because the mountain of Zion is not prominent in these passages, it is probable that the mountain is not cosmic. Rather, these passages appear to develop beliefs already present in earlier canonical writings, that Zion is the dwelling of God and the home of the righteous and that the valley of Hinnon is a place of fiery abomination.

In two texts, however, the fall of the angels is connected to mountains that are known as sacred in Canaanite lore. In 1 Enoch 13, Enoch is asked by the Watchers, who had sinned with the daughters of men (cf. Gen. 6:1-4), to intercede with God on their behalf.

---

5. E.g., 1 En. 25:4-7; 90:24-42.

> And I went off and sat down at the waters of Dan, in the land of Dan, to the south of the west of Hermon: I read their petition till I fell asleep. And behold a dream came to me, and visions fell down upon me, and I saw visions of chastisement, and a voice came bidding (me) to tell it to the sons of heaven, and reprimand them. And when I awaked, I came unto them, and they were all sitting gathered together, weeping in 'Abelsjāîl, which is between Lebanon and Sênêsêr, with their faces covered. (1 En. 13:7-10a)

The visions came to Enoch in a dream at the waters of Dan, just as Ezekiel had received a revelation at the river Chebar (Ezek. 1:1), and Daniel at the bank of the Great River (Dan. 10:4). Here, the water is on Palestinian soil, and has a special significance. It is likely that the site was chosen with a view to the symbolism of the place. The waters of Dan are at the source of the Jordan, the river of Palestine, and the waters are the base of Hermon, a sacred mountain. These characteristics seem to make it a cosmic site, in the tradition of El's mountain, the source of the Two Rivers, of the Double-Deep, and an appropriate locale for divine-human encounter.[6] When Enoch wakes from his vision, he goes to

---

6. J. T. Milik, "Le Testament de Lévi en Araméen," *RB*, 62 (1955), 405. Milik in the same article has made the brilliant suggestion that Matt. 16:12-30, Jesus' promise to build his church on the rock and to protect it from the gates of Hades is uttered on this same spot, and that perhaps the Transfiguration takes place here as well, Matt. 17:1-9 (p. 405, n. 2).

the Watchers who have left the high heaven (12:4) and are sitting in Abel-Maim,[7] which is between Lebanon and Senir, the designation of Hermon.

The Aramaic text of the Testament of Levi of about 100 B.C., discovered at Qumran, makes possible a more precise understanding of the Testament of Levi 2:3-5, a text similar to the Enoch passage. In this text, Levi was feeding the flocks at Abel-Maim, where Enoch had his vision. The spirit of the Lord comes upon him and he prays to the Lord. There follows a prayer for deliverance (contained in one Greek manuscript). Then Levi finds himself upon a high mountain where he sees the heavens opened. According to Milik's restored Aramaic text, "And I saw the heavens opened and I saw below me a high mountain which touched the heavens and I was upon it. And the gates of heaven were opened to me and an angel said to me. . ."[8]

---

7. The name is variously spelled, Greek ΕΒΕΛΣΑΤΑ < ΕΒΕΛΣΑΙΛ, Ethiopic *ʾAbelsyaʾil*. The *mem* could be confused with the *samek* in the writing of the second and first centuries B.C., so Milik, "Le Testament de Lévi," p. 404, n. 3. Abel-Main is Abel-beth-maachah of the monarchic period, about four miles west of the site of Dan. We adopt the evidence of the Aramaic *ʾbl myn*.

8. The restored text: wḥzyt šm[yʾ ptyḥyn wḥzyt ṭwrʾ] tḥwty rm ʿḍ dbq lšm[yʾ whwyt bh wʾtptḥw] ly trʿy šmyʾ wmlʾk hd [ʾmr ly . . .], Milik, "Le Testament de Lévi," p. 404. The same mountain, Sirion, Hermon, is apparently mentioned in the Greek text of the Testament of Levi, 6:1. The Greek translator has misunderstood *Siryōn*. So Milik, ibid.

In Chapter III it has been observed that traditions of sacred mountains adhered to a number of mountains in Canaan: Zaphon-Casios, Hermon, Baal-Zaphon in Egypt, and Zion. The evidence of the last quoted text from 1 Enoch and the Testament of Levi suggests that the tradition of the great battle at the mountain, which the Ugaritic texts place at Zaphon (and Lebanon in one text) and the Hebrew Bible at Zion, also found a home at Mount Hermon. The fallen heavenly creatures, it may be conjectured, have been cast down to the base of the cosmic mountain. Enoch, or Levi, can conveniently intercede for them by ascending from the fallen Watchers to the deity who dwells above. In one Ugaritic text, Anat binds the dragon to the heights of Lebanon (*PRU*, II, 3.8-10). The monster Typhon is buried at the base of Baal-Zaphon in Egypt, according to a local tradition recorded by Herodotus. If the conjecture is valid, the defeated heavenly Watchers are imprisoned at the base of the sacred mountain which they once tried to storm.

The intertestamental literature has provided only slight evidence for the sacred mountain as it has been understood in the previous two chapters. Jerusalem (and Mount Zion) are the central points in legendary geography. Only Mount Hermon seems to be the bearer in intertestamental times of ancient traditions of the holy mountain.

CONCLUSION

It has been seen that mountains played an important role in the religious thought of the Ancient Near East of the first and second millennia. The term sometimes used to describe the holy mountain in English, cosmic mountain, has been based on a postulated Mesopotamian *Weltberg*, or "world-mountain." In this view, heaven and earth united were seen as a mountain. The base of the mountain was the earth and the peak was the top of the heavens. Thus the mountain was the central axis of the universe and was the connecting point between the different spheres. This concept, an assumption of an older generation of Assyriologists, was often applied in an unexamined way to West Semitic and biblical texts. It finds little support in Sumerian and Akkadian texts or in Mesopotamian geography. There is indeed some Mesopotamian evidence for a cosmic center--particularly at Nippur and Babylon. There is no evidence for a cosmic mountain, or *Weltberg*.

Sacred mountains are important, however, among West Semitic peoples in Syria-Palestine. Even if a Mesopotamian *Weltberg* may not be transferred to the religious beliefs of these peoples, the term "cosmic" may nonetheless be retained to describe their sacred mountains. The holy mountains about which there is evidence among the people of Canaan are not merely geographical heights sacred in a vague way. Their sacredness arises from specific beliefs. The mountain could be the meeting place of the divine assembly. Under the presidency of El, the high god, decisions were made about divine power which affected the order and running of the cosmos and the life of the individual believer. The fertile power of the earth clearly was bound up with the mountain. The shifting balance between rainfall and lack of rainfall was decided here. Here was the source of life-giving rivers and the underground waters which fed the wells and springs. The conflict evident in life was a reflection of primal events on the mountain. The mountains were cosmic in these senses.

In Canaan, in the Ugaritic texts reflecting second millennium beliefs, El's mountain is the dwelling place where the divine assembly meets, where the fertilizing waters meet and flow outward, where El, a splendid patriarchal figure, issues authoritative decrees. Baal, the Storm-god, also lives on a mountain, a less serene place. Here Baal had to withstand attacks from monstrous enemies until he could stand as king on his mountain. Baal's kingship was commemorated and made effective by the great temple/palace built on the mountain.

Elements of the Canaanite traditions of the mountain of El have influenced Israelite traditions of Sinai. Sinai is a mountain where Yahweh issues his decrees, although the divine assembly plays no role in the Exodus traditions. On Sinai, Yahweh has his tent, and the earthly copy of the tent, the "Tent of Meeting," mediates Yahweh's presence to his people.

Baal's mountain, Zaphon, has come *nominatim* into Israelite religion. The process whereby traditions of Zaphon have attached themselves to other mountains and hills along the eastern Mediterranean littoral, a process we have termed *translatio*, can actually be traced. Mount Zion in Jerusalem becomes the repository of some Zaphon traditions--those telling of the monstrous attacks on the mountain which remains ultimately impregnable and those which describe the celebration of kingship, won in battle, by the erection of a temple and by a storm theophany. Mount Zion becomes the new Zaphon. In addition, tantalizing fragments telling of a revolt in the heavens against El have entered Israelite tradition.

Jerusalem becomes dominant as a religious symbol in the period of the Second Temple. Paucity of source material makes it difficult to trace in this later literature the outworking of the motifs mentioned above. The omphalos, or navel of the earth, known among the Greeks, comes to be used of Jerusalem. Semimythic geographical texts place Mount Zion in the center of the world. Other texts mention Jerusalem and Mount Hermon as the places where the fallen angels are imprisoned, at the foot of the mountain.

Synoptic Table of Various Systems of Designating Texts

Gordon	*Virolleaud*	*Eissfeldt*	*CTA*
a	"	49	"
b	"	50	"
1	RS 1929, n° 1	1	34
2	RS 1929, n° 2	2	32
3	RS 1929, n° 3	3	35
4	RS 1929, n° 4	4	166
5	RS 1929, n° 5	5	33
6	RS 1929, n° 6	6	13
7	RS 1929, n° 7	7	168
8	RS 1929, n° 8	8	27
9	RS 1929, n° 9	9	36
10	RS 1929, n° 10	10	101
11	RS 1929, n° 11	11	98
12	RS 1929, n° 12	12	142
13	RS 1929, n° 13	13	54
14	RS 1929, n° 14	14	31
15	RS 1929, n° 15	15	107
16	RS 1929, n° 16	16	112
17	RS 1929, n° 17	17	29
18	RS 1929, n° 18	18	55
19	RS 1929, n° 19	19	39
20	RS 1929, n° 20	20	58
21	RS 1929, n° 21	21	56
22	RS 1929, n° 22	22	37
23	RS 1929, n° 23	23	38
24	RS 1929, n° 24	24	199
25	RS 1929, n° 25	25	151

Gordon	*Virolleaud*	*Eissfeldt*	*CTA*
26	RS 1929, n° 26	26	62
27	RS 1929, n° 27	27	180
28	RS 1929, n° 28	28	170
29	RS 1929, n° 29	29	130
30	RS 1929, n° 30	30	183
31	RS 1929, n° 31	31	175
32	RS 1929, n° 32	32	60
33	RS 1929, n° 33	33	47
34	RS 1929, n° 34	34	169
35	RS 1929, n° 35	35	170
36	RS 1929, n° 36	36	150
37	RS 1929, n° 37	37	196
38	RS 1929, n° 38	38	108
39	RS 1929, n° 39	39	211
40	RS 1929, n° 40	40	212
41	RS 1929, n° 41	41	138
42	RS 1929, n° 42	42	195
43	RS 1929, n° 43	43	54
44	RS 1929, n° 44	44	44
45	RS 1929, n° 45	45	169
46	RS 1929, n° 46	46	45
47	RS 1929, n° 47	47	43
48	RS 1929, n° 48	48	194
49	I AB	I AB	6(I AB)
50	"	52	172
51	II AB	II AB	4(II AB)
52	SS	SS	23(SS)
53	53	53	30
54	"	54	53

Gordon	*Virolleaud*	*Eissfeldt*	*CTA*
55	53	55	160
56	"	56	161
57	"	57	207
58	"	58	158
59	"	59	159
60	PS	60	179
61	"	61	176
62	I AB I,1*-29* VI, 38-57	I AB I,1*-29 VI, 38-57	6(I AB), I, 1-29 VI, 38-57
63	"	62	77
64	TG	63	87
65	TG[A]	64	68
66	TG[B]	65	100
67	I* AB	I* AB	5(I* AB)
68	III AB A	III AB A	2 (III AB),IV
69	"	66	"
70	"	67	"
71	"	68	41
72	"	69	48
73	"	70	49
74	"	71	187
75	BH	BH	12 (BH)
76	IV AB	IV AB	10(IV AB)
77	NK	NK	24 (NK)
78: *v.* ‘nt			
79: *v.* ‘nt			
80	"	72	85
81	"	73	75
82	"	74	76

Gordon	*Virolleaud*	*Eissfeldt*	*CTA*
83	NK	75	79
84	"	76	136
85	"	77	83
86	"	78	105
87	"	79	146
88: *v.* ʻnt			
89	T1 I	80	52
90	"	81	147
91	"	82	95
92	"	83 A	137
93	"	83 B	
94	"	84	206
95	T1 II	85	51
96	"	86	148
97	RS 1929, n° 12	12	142
98	"	87	140
99	"	88	149
100	"	89	59
101	"	90	57
102	"	91	165
103	"	92	162
104	"	93	163
105	"	94	164
106	"	95	167
107: v. 53			
108	"	96	65
109	"	97	66
110	"	98	67
111	"	99	69

Gordon	*Virolleaud*	*Eissfeldt*	*CTA*
112	RS 1929, n° 12	100	70
113	"	101	71
114	"	102	73
115	"	103	74
116	"	104	157
117	"	105	50
118	"	106	64
119	"	107	80
120	"	108	141
121(= 4 Aqht)	I Rp.(= IV D)	I Rp.	20(I Rp.)
122	II Rp.	II Rp.	21(II Rp.)
123	III Rp.,A	III Rp.,A	22(III Rp.),A
124	III Rp.,B	III Rp.,B	22(III Rp.),B
125	II K,I-II	II K, I-II	16(II K), I-II
126	II K,III-V	II K,III-V	16(II K),III-V
127	II K,VI	II K,VI	16(II K),VI
128	III K	III K,I-VI	15(III K)
129	III AB, C	III AB,C	2(III AB),III(?)
130	"	V AB, *var.*A	7,II
131	"	V AB, *var.*B	7,I
132	"	IV AB,III*	11
133	"	IMF	9
134	"	145	40
135	"	II MF	26
136	"	III MF	25
137	III AB, B	III AB,B	2(III AB),I
138	"	146	"
300	"	109	82
301	"	110	115

Gordon	*Virolleaud*	*Eissfeldt*	*CTA*
302	III AB, B	111	92
303	"	112	116
304	"	113	88
305	"	114	86
306	"	115	118
307	"	116	121
308	"	117	122
309	"	118	131
310	"	119	139
311	"	120	91
312	"	121	89
313	"	122	94
314	"	123	90
315	"	124	97
316	"	125	104
317	"	126	144
318	"	127	145
319	"	128	84
320	"	129	186
321	"	130	119
322	"	131	102
323	"		
324	"	132	114
325	"	133	117
326	"	134	123
327	"	135	99
328	"	136	93
329	"	137	81
330	"	138	135

Gordon	*Virolleaud*	*Eissfeldt*	*CTA*
331	III AB,B	139	132
332	"	140	106
333	"	141	96
334	"	142	103
335	"	143	153
400	ES	144	113
1 Aqht	I D	I D	19(I D)
2 Aqht	II D	II D	17(II D)
3 Aqht	III D	III D	18(III D)
4 Aqht: *v.* 121			
Krt	I K	I K	14(I K)
ʻnt	V AB	V AB	3(V AB)
ʻnt,pl. IX-X	VI AB	VI AB	1(VI AB)

BIBLIOGRAPHY

INDEXES

A SELECTED BIBLIOGRAPHY

I. *Texts and Primary Archaeological Publications of Ras Shamra*

Donner, H., and W. Röllig. *Kanaänische und Aramäische Inschriften*, 2nd ed. 3 vols. Wiesbaden: Otto Harrassowitz, 1968.

Gordon, Cyrus H. *Ugaritic Textbook*. Rome: Pontifical Biblical Institute, 1965.

Herdner, Andrée. *Corpus des tablettes en cunéiformes alphabétiques*. 2 vols. Paris: Imprimerie Nationale. 1963.

Nougayrol, J. *Le Palais royal d'Ugarit*. Vols. III, IV. Paris: Imprimerie Nationale, 1955, 1956.

Schaeffer, Cl. F. A. *Ugaritica*. Vols. I-V. Paris: Imprimerie Nationale, 1939-1968.

Virolleaud, Charles. *Le Palais royal d'Ugarit*. Vols. II, V. Paris: Imprimerie Nationale, 1957, 1965.

II. *Complete or Extensive Translations of the Ugaritic Texts*

Aistleitner, J. *Die mythologischen und kultischen Texte aus Ras Shamra*, 2nd ed. Budapest: Akadémiai Kiadó, 1965.

Cassuto, Umberto. *The Goddess Anath*. In Hebrew. Jerusalem: The Bialik Institute, 1965.

Driver, G. R. *Canaanite Myths and Legends.* Edinburgh: T. & T. Clark, 1956.

Ginsberg, H. L. "Ugaritic Myths, Epics and Legends," *ANET*, 3rd ed. James B. Pritchard, ed. Princeton, N. J.: Princeton University, 1969. Pp. 129-155.

Gordon, Cyrus H. *Ugaritic Literature.* Rome: Pontifical Biblical Institute, 1949.

Gray, John. *The Legacy of Canaan*, 2nd ed. Leiden: Brill, 1965.

III. *Books and Articles*

Aistleitner, J. "Ein Opfertext aus Ugarit (No. 53) mit Exkurs über kosmologische Beziehungen der Ugaritischen Mythologie," *Acta Orientalia Academiae Scientiarum Hungaricae*, 5 (1955), 1-23.

________ *Wörterbuch der Ugaritischen Sprache*, 3rd ed. O. Eissfeldt, ed. Berlin: Akademie-Verlag, 1967.

Albright, W. F. *Archeology and the Religion of Israel*, 3rd ed. Baltimore: The Johns Hopkins Press, 1953.

________ "Baal-Zephon," *Festschrift Alfred Bertholet.* Tübingen: J. C. B. Mohr, 1950. Pp. 1-14.

________ "A Catalogue of Early Hebrew Lyric Poems," *HUCA*, 23 (1950), 1-39.

________ "The Furniture of El in Canaanite Mythology," *BASOR*, 91 (1943), 39-44.

________ "In Reply to Dr. Gaster's Observations," *BASOR*, 93 (1944), 23-25.

________ "The Mouth of the Rivers," *American Journal of Semitic Languages and Literature*, 35 (1919), 161-195.

________ *The Proto-Sinaitic Inscriptions and Their Decipherment.* Cambridge, Mass.: Harvard University Press, 1966.

________ "The Psalm of Habakkuk," *Studies in Old Testament Prophecy*. H. H. Rowley, ed. Edinburgh: T. & T. Clark, 1950. Pp. 1-18.

________ *Yahweh and the Gods of Canaan*. Garden City, N. Y.: Doubleday, 1968.

Alfrink, Bernard. "Der Versammlungsberg im äussersten Norden (Is 14)," *Biblica*, 14 (1933), 41-67.

Camp de Mertzenfield, E. de. *Inventaire commenté des ivoires phéniciens et apparentes decouverts dans le Proche Orient*. 2 vols. Paris: E. de Boccard, 1954.

Caspari, Wilhelm. "ṭabur (Nabel)," *ZDMG*, 11 (1933), 49-65.

Cassuto, Umberto. *A Commentary on the Book of Exodus*, trans. Israel Abrahams. Jerusalem: The Magnes Press, 1967.

________ *A Commentary on the Book of Genesis*, trans. Israel Abrahams. Jerusalem: The Magnes Press, 1961.

Causse, A. "Le Mythe de la nouvelle Jérusalem du Deutéro-Ésaie à la IIIe Sibylle," *RHPR*, 18 (1938), 377-414.

Charles, R. H. *The Apocrypha and Pseudepigrapha of the Old Testament*. 2 vols. Oxford: Clarendon, 1913.

Child, Brevard. *Myth and Reality in the Old Testament*. Napierville, Ill.: Allenson, 1960.

Clapham, L. R. "Sanchuniathon: The First Two Cycles," unpub. diss., Harvard University, 1969.

Clements, R. E. *God and Temple*. Oxford: Blackwell, 1965.

Cross, F. M., Jr. "The Divine Warrior in Israel's Early Cult," *Biblical Motifs*. Studies and Texts III. A. Altmann, ed. Cambridge, Mass.: Harvard University Press, 1966. Pp. 11-30.

________ "Yahweh and the God of the Patriarchs," *HTR*, 55 (1962), 225-259.

________ "The Song of the Sea and Canaanite Myth," *Journal for Theology and the Church,* 5. New York: Harper, 1968, pp. 1-25.

________ "Studies in Ancient Yahwistic Poetry," unpub. diss., Johns Hopkins, 1950.

Dahood, M. *Psalms I.* Anchor Bible 16. Garden City, N. Y.: Doubleday, 1965.

________ *Psalms II.* Anchor Bible 17. Garden City, N. Y.: Doubleday, 1968.

________ *Ugaritic-Hebrew Philology.* Rome: Pontifical Biblical Institute, 1965.

Dijk, H. J. van. *Ezekiel's Prophecy on Tyre.* Rome: Pontifical Biblical Institute, 1968.

Dulles, Avery. "Symbol, Myth, and the Biblical Revelation," *Theological Studies,* 27 (1966), 1-26.

Eissfeldt, Otto. "Baʻal Ṣaphon von Ugarit und Amon von Ägypten," *Kleine Schriften IV.* Tübingen: J. C. B. Mohr, 1968. Pp. 53-57.

________ *Baal Zaphon, Zeus Casios, und der Durchzug der Israeliten durchs Meer.* Halle: Niemeyer, 1932.

Eliade, Mircea. *Cosmos and History: The Myth of the Eternal Return,* trans. W. R. Trask. New York: Pantheon, 1959.

________ *Images and Symbols,* trans. Philip Mairet. New York: Sheed & Ward, 1961.

________ *Patterns in Comparative Religion,* trans. Rosemary Sheed. New York: World, 1963.

Fitzmyer, J. A. *The Aramaic Inscriptions of Sefire.* Rome: Pontifical Biblical Institute, 1967.

Frankfort, Henri. *Cylinder Seals.* London: Gregg, 1965, reprint of 1939 ed.

________ ed. *Before Philosophy*. Hammondsworth: Penguin, 1949.

Friedrich, Johannes, and Wolfgang Röllig. *Phönizisch-Punische Grammatik*. 2nd ed. Analecta Orientalia 46. Rome: Pontifical Biblical Institute, 1970.

Gaster, T. H. "The Furniture of El in Canaanite Mythology," *BASOR*, 93 (1944), 20-23.

________ *Thespis*, rev. ed. New York: Doubleday, 1961.

Grelot, Pierre. "Isaie xiv 12-15 et son arrière-plan mythologique," *RHR*, 149 (1956), 18-48.

Gröndahl, Frauke. *Die Personennamen der Texte aus Ugarit*. Rome: Pontifical Biblical Institute, 1967.

Güterbock, H. G. *Kumarbi*. New York: Europaverlag, 1946.

Haussig, H. W., ed. *Wörterbuch der Mytholgie*, vol. I: *Götter und Mythen im Vorderen Orient*. Stuttgart: Ernst Klett, 1965.

Hayes, J. H. "The Tradition of Zion's Inviolability," *JBL*, 82 (1963), 419-426.

Jacobsen, Thorkild. "The Battle between Marduk and Tiamat," *JAOS*, 88 (1968), 104-108.

________ "Primitive Democracy in Mesopotamia," *JNES*, 2 (1943), 159-172.

________ "Sumerian Mythology: A Review Article," *JNES*, 5 (1946), 128-152.

________ *Toward the Image of Tammuz and Other Essays on Mesopotamian History and Culture*, ed. W. L. Moran. Cambridge, Mass.: Harvard University Press, 1970.

Jean, Charles, and Jacob Hoftijzer. *Dictionnaire des Inscriptions semitiques de l'ouest*. Leiden: Brill, 1965.

Jeremias, Johannes. *Der Gottesberg*. Gütersloh: C. Bertelmann, 1919.

Kaiser, Otto. *Die mythische Bedeutung des Meeres im Ägypten, Ugarit, und Israel,* 2nd ed. BZAW, 78. Berlin: Alfred Töpelmann, 1962.

Kramer, S. N. "Dilmun, the Land of the Living," *BASOR*, 96 (1944), 18-28.

________ ed. *Mythologies of the Ancient World.* Garden City, N. Y.: Doubleday, 1961.

________ *Sumerian Mythology*, rev. ed. Torchbook. New York: Harper, 1961.

Kraus, H. J. *Psalmen.* BK XV. Neukirchen-Vluyn: Verlag der Buchhandlung des Erziehungsverein, 1960.

________ *Worship in Israel,* trans. G. Buswell. Richmond, Va.: John Knox, 1966.

Kristensen, W. Brede. *The Meaning of Religion,* trans. John B. Carman. The Hague: Martinus Nijhoff, 1960.

Landsberger, B., and J. V. Kinnier Wilson, "The Fifth Tablet of *Enūma elīš*," *JNES*, 20 (1961), 154-179.

Langhe, Robert de. *Les Textes de Ras Shamra-Ugarit et leurs Rapports avec le Milieu Biblique de l'Ancien Testament.* Paris: Desclée de Brouwer, 1945.

Lipínski, E. "Juges 5, 4-5 et Psaume 68, 8-11," *Biblica,* 48 (1967), 185-206.

Milik, J. T. "Hénoch au pays des Aromates," *RB*, 65 (1958), 70-77.

________ "Le Testament de Lévi en Araméen," *RB*, 62 (1955), 398-406.

Miller, Patrick D. "El the Warrier," *HTR*, 60 (1967), 411-431.

Mowinckel, Sigmund. *The Psalms in Israel's Worship,* trans. D. R. Ap-Thomas. New York: Abingdon, 1967.

Neuberg, F. "An Unrecognized Meaning of Hebrew *Dôr*," *JNES,* 9 (1950), 215-217.

Ohler, Annemarie. *Mythologische Elemente im Alten Testament*. Dusseldorf: Patmos, 1969.

Otten, Heinrich. "Ein kanaanäischer Mythus aus Boğasköy," *MIO* (1953), pp. 125-150.

Parrot, André. *Ziqqurats et Tour de Babel*. Paris: Albin Michel, 1949.

Peckham, J. Brian. *The Development of the Late Phoenician Scripts*. Cambridge, Mass.: Harvard University Press, 1968.

Pope, Marvin. *El in the Ugaritic Texts*. Supplements to Vetus Testamentum II. Leiden: Brill, 1955.

Pritchard, James B., ed. *The Ancient Near East in Pictures*. 2nd ed. Princeton, N. J.: Princeton University, 1969.

________ *Ancient Near Eastern Texts*. 3rd ed. Princeton, N. J.: Princeton University, 1969.

Russell, D. S. *The Method & Message of Jewish Apocalyptic*. Philadelphia: Westminster, 1964.

Schaeffer, Cl. F. A. *The Cuneiform Texts of Ras Shamra-Ugarit*. London: Oxford, 1939.

Schmid, Herbert. "Jahwe und die Kulttraditionen von Jerusalem," *ZAW*, 26 (1955), 168-197.

Schmidt, K. L. "Jerusalem als Urbild und Abbild," *Eranos Jahrbuch*. Vol. 18. Olga Fröbe-Kapteyn, ed. Zurich: Rhein Verlag, 1950. Pp. 207-248.

Schmidt, Werner. *Königtum Gottes in Ugarit und Israel*, 2nd ed. BZAW, 80. Berlin: Alfred Töpelmann, 1966.

Seeligmann, J. H. "Jerusalem in Jewish-Hellenistic Thought," *Judah and Jerusalem:* The Twelfth Annual Archeological Convention. Jerusalem: Israel Exploration Society, 1957. Pp. 192-208. In Hebrew.

Sjöberg, Åke W., and E. Bergmann. *The Collection of the Sumerian Temple Hymns*. Locust Valley: J. J. Augustin, 1969.

Speiser, E. A. "Akkadian Myths and Epics," *ANET*, 1969. Pp. 60-119.

_________ "*Ēd* in the Story of Creation," *Oriental and Biblical Studies*. J. J. Finkelstein and M. Greenberg, ed. Philadelphia: University of Pennsylvania, 1967. Pp. 19-22.

_________ "The Rivers of Paradise," *Oriental and Biblical Studies*. J. J. Finkelstein and M. Greenberg, ed. Philadelphia: University of Pennsylvania, 1967. Pp. 23-34.

Terrien, Samuel. "The Omphalos Myth and Hebrew Religion," *VT*, 20 (1970), 315-338.

Tromp, N. J. *Primitive Conceptions of Death and the Netherworld in the Old Testament*. Rome: Pontifical Biblical Institute, 1969.

Van Buren, E. Douglas. *Symbols of the Gods in Mesopotamia*. Rome: Pontifical Biblical Institute, 1945.

Van der Leeuw, G. *Religion in Essence and Manifestation*, trans. J. E. Turner with additions of 2nd German edition. London: Allen & Unwin, 1938.

Vaux, Roland de. *Ancient Israel*, trans. J. McHugh. New York: McGraw-Hill, 1961.

_________ "Arche d'Alliance et Tente de Réunion," *Bible et Orient*. Paris: Cerf, 1967. Pp. 261-276.

_________ "Jerusalem and the Prophets," *Interpreting the Prophetic Tradition*. The Goldenson Lectures 1955-1966. New York: KTAV, 1969.

Von Soden, W. "Gibt es ein Zeugnis dafür, dass die Babylonier an die Wiederauferstehung Marduks geglaubt haben?" *ZA*, NS, 17 (1955), 130-166.

Wales, H. G. Qaritch. *The Mountain of God: A Study in Early Kingship*. London: Bernard Quaritch, 1953.

Wanke, Gunther. *Die Zionstheologie der Korachiten*. BZAW, 97. Berlin: Alfred Töpelmann, 1966.

Watson, Paul. "Mot, the God of Death, at Ugarit and in the Old Testament," unpub. diss., Yale University, 1970.

Weiser, Artur. *The Psalms*, trans. H. Hartwell. Philadelphia, Westminster, 1962.

Westermann, Claus. *Genesis*. BK I. Neukirchen-Vluyn: Verlag des Erziehungsverein, 1970.

Wildberger, Hans. *Jesaja*. BK X. Neukirchen-Vluyn: Verlag des Erziehungsverein, 1965.

Wright, G. Ernest. *Biblical Archaeology*, 2nd ed. Philadelphia: Westminster, 1962.

_________ "Sinai, Mount," *IDB*. New York: Abingdon, 1962. IV, 376-378.

Zimmerli, Walther. *Ezechiel*. BK XIII. Neukirchen-Vluyn: Verlag des Erziehungsverein, 1969.

BIBLICAL REFERENCES

SUBJECT INDEX